1st EDITION

Perspectives on Diseases and Disorders

Neurodegenerative Disorders

Sylvia Engdahl
Book Editor

Detroit • New York • San Francisco • New Haven, Conn • Waterville, Maine • London

Elizabeth Des Chenes, *Director, Publishing Solutions*

For more information, contact:
Greenhaven Press
27500 Drake Rd.
Farmington Hills, MI 48331-3535
Or you can visit our Internet site at gale.cengage.com

For product information and technology assistance, contact us at

Gale Customer Support, 1-800-877-4253
For permission to use material from this text or product, submit all requests online at www.cengage.com/permissions

Further permissions questions can be e-mailed to permissionrequest@cengage.com

LIBRARY OF CONGRESS CATALOGING-IN-PUBLICATION DATA

Neurodegenerative disorders / Sylvia Engdahl, book editor.
    pages cm -- (Perspectives on diseases and disorders)
  Summary: "Perspectives on Diseases and Disorders: Neurodegenerative Disorders: Each volume in this timely series provides essential information on a disease or disorder (symptoms, causes, treatments, cures, etc.); presents the controversies surrounding causes, alternative treatments, and other issues"-- Provided by publisher.
  Includes bibliographical references and index.
  ISBN 978-0-7377-6357-7 (hardback)
 1. Nervous system--Degeneration. I. Engdahl, Sylvia, editor of compilation.
  RC365.N462 2013
  616.8'0442--dc23
                                         2012035624

Printed in the United States of America
1 2 3 4 5 6 7 16 15 14 13 12

CONTENTS

Institute for Neurological Discoveries

Neurodegenerative diseases involve the failure
and death of nerve cells in the brain, spinal cord,
or peripheral nerves. They come on gradually,
and the symptoms worsen. Although the various
neurodegenerative disorders are considered distinct,
in practice there is a great deal of overlap between
them, so they are difficult to diagnose.

Anne Brown Rodgers

There are billions of neurons in the human brain,
which communicate with each other and the rest
of the body by means of fibers called axons and
dendrites. They all have special jobs—for example,
some are involved with thinking and some control
muscles. Scientists study normal age-related changes
in neurons to learn more about neurodegenerative
disorders.

symptoms of them overlap and differ in individual patients, the lines between them are not clear. Also, the specific damage by which these diseases are defined may not be the primary cause of a person's symptoms. Many doctors now think they should not be viewed as discrete conditions.

learning to use stem cells from adults. One of the most promising uses for adult stem cells is to replace neurons destroyed by neurodegenerative diseases such as Parkinson's disease and Huntington's disease. If this can be done, it may become possible to treat these disorders.

been approved by the FDA and cannot be offered in the United States, many are traveling to foreign countries to receive it. Scientists are skeptical about this theory, and it will take years for researchers to learn whether it is valid.

objections to someone with a serious disease flying in space. Since retiring, he has gone public to inspire others with Parkinson's.

FOREWORD

"Medicine, to produce health, has to examine disease."
—Plutarch

Independent research on a health issue is often the first step to complement discussions with a physician. But locating accurate, well-organized, understandable medical information can be a challenge. A simple Internet search on terms such as "cancer" or "diabetes," for example, returns an intimidating number of results. Sifting through the results can be daunting, particularly when some of the information is inconsistent or even contradictory. The Greenhaven Press series Perspectives on Diseases and Disorders offers a solution to the often overwhelming nature of researching diseases and disorders.

From the clinical to the personal, titles in the Perspectives on Diseases and Disorders series provide students and other researchers with authoritative, accessible information in unique anthologies that include basic information about the disease or disorder, controversial aspects of diagnosis and treatment, and first-person accounts of those impacted by the disease. The result is a well-rounded combination of primary and secondary sources that, together, provide the reader with a better understanding of the disease or disorder.

Each volume in Perspectives on Diseases and Disorders explores a particular disease or disorder in detail. Material for each volume is carefully selected from a wide range of sources, including encyclopedias, journals, newspapers, nonfiction books, speeches, government documents, pamphlets, organization newsletters, and position papers. Articles in the first chapter provide an authoritative, up-to-date overview that covers symptoms, causes and effects, treatments, cures, and medical advances. The second chapter presents a substantial number of opposing viewpoints on controversial treatments and other current debates relating to the volume topic. The third chapter offers a variety of personal perspectives on the disease or disorder. Patients, doctors, caregivers, and loved ones represent just some of the voices found in this narrative chapter.

Each Perspectives on Diseases and Disorders volume also includes:

- An **annotated table of contents** that provides a brief summary of each article in the volume.
- An **introduction** specific to the volume topic.
- Full-color **charts and graphs** to illustrate key points, concepts, and theories.
- Full-color **photos** that show aspects of the disease or disorder and enhance textual material.
- **"Fast Facts"** that highlight pertinent additional statistics and surprising points.
- A **glossary** providing users with definitions of important terms.
- A **chronology** of important dates relating to the disease or disorder.
- An annotated list of **organizations to contact** for students and other readers seeking additional information.
- A **bibliography** of additional books and periodicals for further research.
- A detailed **subject index** that allows readers to quickly find the information they need.

Whether a student researching a disorder, a patient recently diagnosed with a disease, or an individual who simply wants to learn more about a particular disease or disorder, a reader who turns to Perspectives on Diseases and Disorders will find a wealth of information in each volume that offers not only basic information, but also vigorous debate from multiple perspectives.

INTRODUCTION

The functioning of the human body and mind is controlled by the nervous system, which consists of billions of nerve cells called neurons and the connections between them. When something goes wrong in the body, causing a significant number of its neurons to fail and eventually die, the result is a neurodegenerative disorder; that is, a disorder or disease characterized by the degeneration of neurons.

There are hundreds of neurodegenerative disorders, most of which are rare. They are distinguished by different mechanisms affecting different neurons, but all have many things in common, including:

- They involve the loss of nerve cells in the brain, or in some cases in the spinal cord or peripheral nerves.
- They are physically and/or mentally disabling to one degree or another.
- They are progressive, meaning that the symptoms gradually worsen, although in the case of some there may be periods of remission.
- They are incurable, although for some there are treatments to help manage the symptoms.
- Many of them are fatal, sometimes within a few years.
- Except in the case of genetic disorders passed from one generation to another, their underlying causes are not yet fully understood.
- With rare exception, they are not contagious.
- There is no known way to prevent any of them, despite theories that suggest possible risk factors.

Apart from Alzheimer's disease, which is common in old age, neurodegenerative disorders affect only a small fraction of the population. But because they are generally severe and incapacitating, they cause far more suffering than most other diseases, not only for their victims but for the victims' families, and the burden they impose on society as a whole is high. People with late-stage neurodegenerative diseases cannot engage in the routine activities of daily living without help from special technologies and/or from full-time caregivers. In some cases they are unable to move their limbs or even to speak or eat. In others, their memories fail, and they are unable to think clearly or to recognize loved ones. With a disease that is quickly fatal, this incapacity may last only a little while, but with diseases that take a long time to progress, it may continue for many years.

Neurodegenerative diseases can be roughly divided into two main types: those that affect cognition and those that affect motor abilities (some, however, affect both). Examples of those that affect primarily cognition include Alzheimer's disease, frontotemporal dementia, and Lewy body dementia. Among those that affect primarily motor abilities are Parkinson's disease, amyotrophic lateral sclerosis (ALS, often called Lou Gehrig's disease), and multiple sclerosis.

Traditionally, the many neurodegenerative disorders have been considered separate diseases, and they all have names that distinguish them. However, their symptoms often overlap so that they are often very difficult to diagnose. This is true because mild, even unnoticeable, symptoms appear first, and it may be years before the pattern of a person's disabilities becomes evident. Moreover, the specific type of damage to neurons cannot always be determined by tests; sometimes, in fact, it can be seen only during autopsy. So diagnosis often depends more on ruling out other possibilities than on finding identifying evidence, and misdiagnosis is not unusual. For these reasons some doctors believe that until such time as effective treatments are found, it would be better not to think of neurodegenerative disorders as discrete entities but rather to view symptoms as a continuum from mild to severe. But disease names are useful so that all researchers will be speaking the same language, and because insurance companies require specific diagnoses when claims are submitted for the costs of treatment.

The neurodegenerative diseases named after people—Alzheimer's, Parkinson's, Huntington's, and the like—bear the names of the physicians who first described them. Lou Gehrig's disease (an unofficial name for ALS), which is known to the public by the name of a well-known baseball player who was a victim of the disease, is an exception.

Some neurodegenerative diseases are inherited, so that it is possible to know in advance the chances that children of affected parents will have them or get them later in life. But most either are not of genetic origin or tend to occur among relatives without any known pattern of inheritance. Those that appear randomly are called sporadic. A few, such as ALS, have both inherited and sporadic forms.

The causes of the sporadic neurodegenerative disorders are not known, although risk factors for some have been identified. The greatest risk factor for most of them, especially those involving dementia, is advancing age. While some neurodegenerative diseases occur in children, the majority appear either in midlife or not until old age—although early signs may sometimes be detectable long before any symptoms appear, as is now often the case with Parkinson's disease. Neurodegenerative diseases are therefore an increasing problem for society because the average lifespan is increasing; more people than in the past are living long enough to get these diseases, and this trend accelerates as more and more other diseases become preventable or curable.

Alzheimer's disease (AD) is an especially serious problem, since it is more common than other neurodegenerative diseases. Currently about 13 percent of people

Neurogenerative diseases such as Alzheimer's and other dementias can affect cognition, whereas Parkinson's disease and amyotrophic lateral sclerosis affect motor abilities. (© **Lisa F. Young/Alamy**)

over the age of sixty-five have it, and nearly 50 percent of those over eighty-five. AD, which is not preventable, is a slow death, generally preceded by years of mental disability due to physical changes in the brain. Senility, meaning the loss of memory and capacity to reason, was once thought to be normal in extreme old age, but it is not—rather, it is the result of AD or some other neurodegenerative disease involving dementia. Families are devastated when this strikes a loved one, and their lives are often further disrupted by providing full-time care or paying the high cost of placing the person in a nursing home. For most, this cost is prohibitive, which means that it has to be paid by the government and is thus a burden not only on families but on all taxpayers. Economists are currently worried by the projected rise in AD cases by the middle of this century; they fear that not enough money can be made available to provide adequate care for all.

So finding a cure for AD—or better yet, a way to prevent it—has a very high priority, and many scientists are searching for such solutions. But the task is not simple. To find a cure or preventative treatment, they must first find the underlying cause of the disease. Researchers know what is wrong in the brains of people with the disease, but there is disagreement as to how much of the visible abnormality is the cause of AD and how much is an effect. In any case, they do not know what triggers it. Even if this is discovered in the near future, the development of drugs to treat the disease or its risk factors will take time.

Meanwhile, the other neurodegenerative disorders are just as cruel to those affected by them, and although fewer people get them, even a tiny percentage of the population adds up to a great many individual victims. For example, it is estimated that thirty thousand to thirty-five thousand Americans have ALS at any given time, and since that is a disease that usually kills within three to five years, over a decade far more are stricken by it. Most people with ALS get it during the prime of life, and they are physically rather than mentally disabled, often unable to move, eat, or speak. They too must have full-time care, and like those with many other incurable diseases that strike before old age, many are vocal in demanding progress toward a cure. Funds for research on neurodegen-erative diseases must be split many ways, though there is hope that what is learned about one such disease may prove applicable to others.

Research that deals with neurons is a great deal more complex than discovery of the microorganisms that cause infectious diseases, against many of which vaccines were developed long ago. Vaccines cannot prevent neurode-generative diseases because entirely different principles of biology are involved. A major breakthrough will be needed before these disorders can be effectively treated by medical science.

Neurodegenerative diseases do not receive as much publicity as cancer, heart disease, or AIDS; yet they are greatly feared. It is true that for anyone under sixty-five the chances of getting such a disease are extremely small, but for those who are affected, the impact is great.

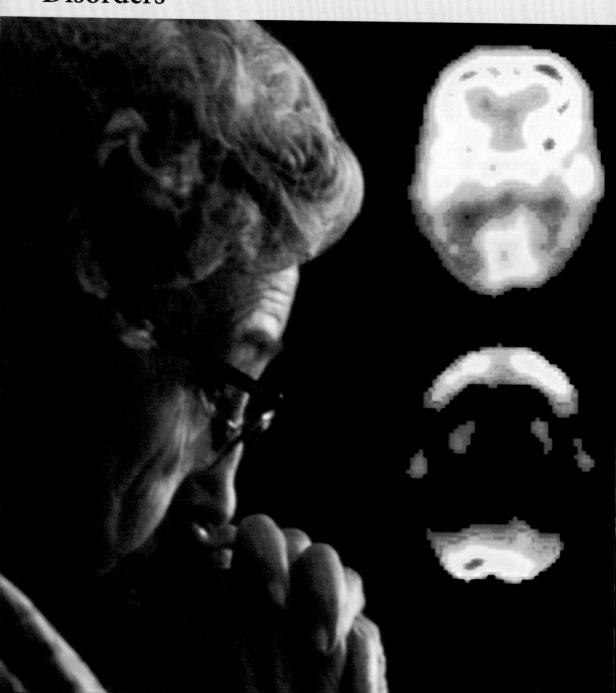

CHAPTER 1

Understanding Neurodegenerative Disorders

Neurodegenerative Disorders Are Progressive Diseases Characterized by Nerve Cell Failure

Institute for Neurological Discoveries

Neurodegenerative diseases begin gradually and keep on getting worse as nerve cells in the brain, spinal cord, or peripheral nerves fail and die. There are many such diseases, categorized by what kinds of symptoms appear first, but because their symptoms overlap they are difficult to diagnose. Also, most of them involve more than one type of nervous system failure. Some neurodegenerative diseases begin in early childhood, others in youth or middle age, and still others mainly in old age. Some are entirely genetic, inherited according to known patterns, while others appear unpredictably. Neurodegenerative diseases of the brain cause memory loss, impaired cognition, personality change, and weakness or problems with movement due to lack of muscle control. Those of the nerves produce problems with strength or sensation and sometimes pain.

The Institute for Neurological Discoveries at the University of Kansas seeks to prevent and cure nervous system diseases.

Photo on facing page. A brain scan of an elderly woman suffering from Alzheimer's disease, bottom, is compared with a normal brain scan (top). (© NARA/ NIH/Jessica Wilson/Photo Researchers, Inc.)

Neurodegenerative diseases are characterized clinically by their insidious [stealthy] onset and chronic progression. Particular parts of the brain, spinal cord, or peripheral nerves functionally fail and the neurons [nerve cells] of the dysfunctional region die. Neuroanatomically localizable functional impairment and neurodegeneration associate with recognizable syndromes that are ideally distinct, although in clinical and even neuropathology practice substantial syndromic overlap exists. Neurodegenerative disease clinical syndromes are often categorized by whether they initially affect cognition, movement, strength, coordination, sensation, or autonomic control. Frequently, however, patients will present with [appear as] symptoms and signs referable to more than one system. Either involvement of several systems can occur concomitantly [incidentally], or else by the time the patient has functionally declined enough to seek medical attention multiple systems have become involved. Diagnosing neurodegenerative diseases can prove particularly intimidating to clinicians, because many times the diagnosis cannot be critically "confirmed" by a simple test.

FAST FACT

All neurodegenerative disorders are incurable. Treatments are available for some that slow their progression or at least help with symptoms, but so far no cures are in sight.

Neurodegenerative diseases are complicated on other levels. While the term "neurodegenerative" implies it is the loss of neurons that cause disease, it is possible neuronal demise is merely the final stage of a preceding period of neuron dysfunction. It is difficult to know whether clinical decline associates with actual neuron loss, or with a period of neuron dysfunction that precedes neuron loss. Also, particular neurodegenerative diseases are etiologically heterogeneous [due to mixed causes]. The manifestations of human nervous system failure, not surprisingly, are limited. This brings up some very real questions of lumping versus splitting.

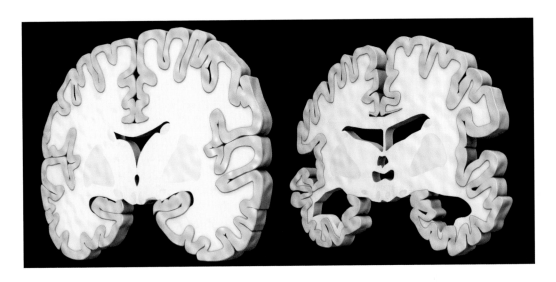

In addition to syndromically defining neurodegenerative diseases by what neuroanatomical system is involved, these disorders are broken down along other clinical lines. Early (childhood, young adulthood, or middle aged adulthood) versus late (old age) onset is an important distinction. Some clinically similar neurodegenerative diseases are sub-categorized by their age of onset, despite the fact at the molecular level different forms of a particular disease may have very little in common. Sporadic onset versus Mendelian [genetic] inheritance constitutes another important distinction, and many named neurodegenerative diseases have both sporadic (Mendelian inheritance is not recognizable) and Mendelian subtypes. . . .

Compared with the computer-generated image of a normal brain on the left, an Alzheimer's-affected brain (right) has enlarged ventricles, or holes within the brain tissue, and deep indentations around the brain's edges. (© Pasieka/Photo Researchers, Inc.)

Degenerative Disorders of the Brain

Degenerative disorders of the brain can present as memory loss, personality change, problems with movement, weakness, or poor balance.

These neurodegenerative diseases can present with memory loss or personality change: Alzheimer's disease, Frontotemporal Dementias, Dementia with Lewy Bodies, Prion diseases.

Neurodegenerative Disorders Affect the Body and Mind in Different Ways

Diseases of the Brain:
Progressive conditions affect the body and mind in different ways.

Alzheimer's symptoms

Cognitive: Memory loss and deterioration in thinking and planning functions.

Physical: In mid-stage, disease could include slowness, rigidity, and tremors.

Parkinson's symptoms

Cognitive: Loss of executive functions, including planning, decision making, and controlling emotions.

Physical: Tremors, stiffness, and slowed movements.

Inside the brain
The cortex, particularly the **hippocampus**, key to memory, shrinks.

Inside the brain
Cells shrink in the substantia nigra, where dopamine is produced.

Ventricles
(fluid-filled spaces within the brain) enlarge.

Lewy bodies
(clusters of alpha-synuclein protein) accumulate inside neurons.

Plaques
(amyloid deposits) cluster between neurons.

Tangles
(twisted proteins) are found within neurons.

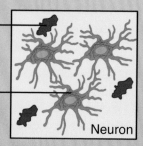

Neuron

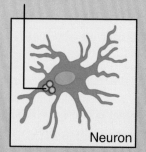

Neuron

These neurodegenerative diseases can present as problems with movements: Parkinson's disease, Huntington's disease, Progressive Supranuclear Palsy, Corticobasal Degeneration, Mutiple System Atrophy.

These neurodegenerative diseases can present as weakness: amyotrophic lateral sclerosis, inclusion body myositis, degenerative myopathies.

These neurodegenerative diseases can present as poor balance: the spinocerebellar atrophies.

Degenerative Disorders of the Nerves

Degenerative disorders of nerves can present as problems with sensation, strength, pain, or autonomic control.

Disorders of the peripheral nerves include diabetic neuropathy, other metabolic neuropathies, endocrine neuropathies, orthostatic hypotension.

Disorders of myelin include multiple sclerosis, Charcot-Marie-Tooth disease [affecting nerves outside the brain and spine].

Researchers Learn About Neurodegenerative Disorders by Studying the Aging Brain

Anne Brown Rodgers

There are billions of neurons in the human brain, connected by fibers called axons and dendrites through which they communicate, typically by the release and reception of chemicals called neurotransmitters. Groups of neurons have specific functions that control the body and mind. Neurons must continually maintain and repair themselves, and as a person gets older changes in the brain occur. Scientists have learned what changes are normal through the investigation of what neurodegenerative diseases do to the brain, and they hope that studying the differences will eventually lead to therapies for age-related neurodegenerative diseases.

Anne Brown Rodgers is a writer and editor specializing in health-related issues.

T he human brain is made up of billions of neurons. Each has a cell body, an axon, and many dendrites. The cell body contains a nucleus, which controls much of the cell's activities. The cell

SOURCE: Anne Brown Rodgers, "Neurons and Their Jobs," *Alzheimer's Disease: Unraveling the Mystery*, National Institute on Aging, pp. 14–15, 17, 41.

body also contains other structures, called organelles, that perform specific tasks.

The axon, which is much narrower than the width of a human hair, extends out from the cell body. Axons transmit messages from neuron to neuron. Sometimes, signal transmissions—like those from head to toe—have to travel over very long distances. Axons are covered with an insulating layer called myelin (also called white matter because of its whitish color). Myelin, which is made by a particular kind of glial cell, increases the speed of nerve signal transmissions through the brain.

Dendrites also branch out from the cell body. They receive messages from the axons of other neurons. Each neuron is connected to thousands of other nerve cells through its axon and dendrites.

Groups of neurons in the brain have special jobs. For example, some are involved with thinking, learning, and memory. Others are responsible for receiving information from the sensory organs (such as the eyes and ears) or the skin. Still others communicate with muscles, stimulating them into action.

Several processes all have to work smoothly together for neurons, and the whole organism, to survive and stay healthy. These processes are communication, metabolism, and repair.

Communication

Imagine the many miles of fiber-optic cables that run under our streets. Day and night, millions of televised and telephonic messages flash at incredible speeds, letting people strike deals, give instructions, share a laugh, or learn some news. Miniaturize it, multiply it many-fold, make it much more complex, and you have the brain. Neurons are the great communicators, always in touch with their neighbors.

Neurons communicate with each other through their axons and dendrites. When a dendrite receives an incoming signal (electrical or chemical), an "action potential," or nerve impulse, can be generated in the cell body. The action potential travels to the end of the axon and once there, the passage of either electrical current or, more typically, the release of chemical messengers, called neurotransmitters, can be triggered. The neurotransmitters are released from the axon terminal and move across a tiny gap, or synapse, to specific receptor sites on the receiving, or post-synaptic, end of dendrites of nearby neurons. A typical neuron has thousands of synaptic connections, mostly on its many dendrites, with other neurons. Cell bodies also have receptor sites for neurotransmitters.

Once the post-synaptic receptors are activated, they open channels through the cell membrane into the receiving nerve cell's interior or start other processes that determine what the receiving nerve cell will do. Some neurotransmitters inhibit nerve cell function (that is, they make it less likely that the nerve cell will send an electrical signal down its axon). Other neurotransmitters stimulate nerve cells, priming the receiving cell to become active or send an electrical signal down the axon to more neurons in the pathway. A neuron receives signals from many other neurons simultaneously, and the sum of a neuron's neurotransmitter inputs at any one instant will determine whether it sends a signal down its axon to activate or inhibit the action of other neighboring neurons.

During any one moment, millions of these signals are speeding through pathways in the brain, allowing the brain to receive and process information, make adjustments, and send out instructions to various parts of the body.

FAST FACT

Aging is the greatest risk factor for most neurodegenerative disorders. It used to be thought that a significant loss of cognitive ability in old age was due to senility, but it is now known that this is not normal but is a manifestation of neurodegenerative disease.

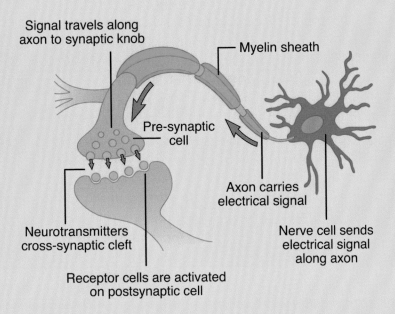

How Nerve Cells Communicate

Signal travels along axon to synaptic knob

Myelin sheath

Pre-synaptic cell

Neurotransmitters cross-synaptic cleft

Axon carries electrical signal

Nerve cell sends electrical signal along axon

Receptor cells are activated on postsynaptic cell

Taken from: Luke Kristopher Davis. "An Exploration into Our Brain and Central Nervous System." *Mattjwaller* (blog), August 4, 2011. www.mattjwaller.com.

Metabolism and Repair

All cells break down chemicals and nutrients to generate energy and form building blocks that make new cellular molecules such as proteins. This process is called metabolism. To maintain metabolism, the brain needs plenty of blood constantly circulating through its billions of capillaries to supply neurons and other brain cells with oxygen and glucose. Without oxygen and glucose, neurons will quickly die.

Nerve cells are formed during fetal life and for a short time after birth. Unlike most cells, which have a fairly short lifespan, neurons in the brain live a long time. These cells can live for up to 100 years or longer. To stay healthy, living neurons must constantly maintain and repair themselves.

In an adult, when neurons die because of disease or injury, they are not usually replaced. Research, however, shows that in a few brain regions, new neurons can be generated, even in the old brain.

Changes in the Brain

In the past several decades, investigators have learned much about what happens in the brain when people have a neurodegenerative disease such as Parkinson's disease, AD [Alzheimer's disease], or other dementias. Their findings also have revealed much about what happens during healthy aging. Researchers are investigating a number of changes related to healthy aging in hopes of learning more about this process so they can fill gaps in our knowledge about the early stages of AD.

As a person gets older, changes occur in all parts of the body, including the brain:

- Certain parts of the brain shrink, especially the prefrontal cortex (an area at the front of the frontal lobe) and the hippocampus. Both areas are important to learning, memory, planning, and other complex mental activities.
- Changes in neurons and neurotransmitters affect communication between neurons. In certain brain regions, communication between neurons can be reduced because white matter (myelin-covered axons) is degraded or lost.
- Changes in the brain's blood vessels occur. Blood flow can be reduced because arteries narrow and less growth of new capillaries occurs.
- In some people, structures called plaques and tangles develop outside of and inside neurons, respectively, although in much smaller amounts than in AD.
- Damage by free radicals increases (free radicals are a kind of molecule that reacts easily with other molecules).

- Inflammation increases (inflammation is the complex process that occurs when the body responds to an injury, disease, or abnormal situation). . . .

Protein Misfolding

Researchers have found that a number of devastating neurodegenerative diseases (for example, AD, Parkinson's disease, dementia with Lewy bodies, frontotemporal lobar degeneration, Huntington's disease, and prion diseases) share a key characteristic—protein misfolding.

When a protein is formed, it "folds" into a unique three-dimensional shape that helps it perform its specific function. This crucial process can go wrong for various reasons, and more commonly does go wrong in aging cells. As a result, the protein folds into an abnormal shape—it is misfolded. . . .

Normally, cells repair or degrade misfolded proteins, but if many of them are formed as part of age-related

In Alzheimer's, changes in the blood vessels cause reduced blood flow. This computerized axial tomography (CAT) scan of a brain with Alzheimer's shows a marked decrease in blood flow in the temporal and parietal lobes. (© Living Art Enterprise, LLC/Photo Researchers, Inc.)

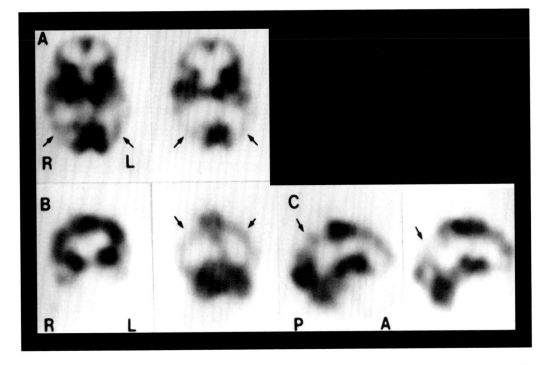

changes, the body's repair and clearance process can be overwhelmed. Misfolded proteins can begin to stick together with other misfolded proteins to form insoluble aggregates. As a result, these aggregates can build up, leading to disruption of cellular communication, and metabolism, and even to cell death. These effects may predispose a person to AD or other neurodegenerative diseases.

Scientists do not know exactly why or how these processes occur, but research into the unique characteristics and actions of various misfolded proteins is helping investigators learn more about the similarities and differences across age-related neurodegenerative diseases. This knowledge may someday lead to therapies. . . .

Neurodegenerative diseases like AD, Parkinson's disease, amyotrophic lateral sclerosis (ALS), and dementia with Lewy bodies share more than the basic characteristic of misfolded proteins. They also share clinical characteristics. For example, people with AD have trouble moving, a characteristic of Parkinson's disease. Sleep-wake disorders, delusions, psychiatric disturbances, and memory loss occur in all of these diseases. These diseases also result from a combination of genetic, lifestyle, and environmental causes and they develop over many years. . . .

By investigating the unique characteristics of these diseases as well as the characteristics they share, scientists hope to learn even more than they would if they focused on each disease by itself.

People with Neurodegenerative Disorders Often Need Long-Term Full-Time Care

World Federation for Mental Health

Caring for a family member who has a neurodegenerative disorder can be rewarding, but it is a difficult and often full-time job. The dementia resulting from many such diseases causes memory loss, confusion, and changes in personality or behavior. People with these diseases may need help in dressing and may become unable to control their bladder or bowels. In the late stages, they may be unable to walk or even sit up by themselves and may have difficulty eating. Those with multiple sclerosis may have some of these symptoms plus weakness, loss of balance, and difficulty speaking. Every case is different, and it is important for caregivers to learn about the usual progression of a specific disease.

The World Federation for Mental Health is an international membership organization that works to advance the prevention of mental and emotional disorders and the proper treatment and care of those with such disorders.

Caring for loved ones with neurological disorders . . . has many positive, life-giving rewards. Many caregivers report tremendous personal satisfaction giving back to those who have given to them. Other caregivers are grateful for a deeper, more meaningful relationship that develops over the course of caregiving. Beyond the personal satisfaction gained from caregiving, the economic impact of caregiving is enormous. Caregivers are the backbone of the long-term care systems in many countries, saving governments millions of dollars each year.

Caring for someone with Alzheimer's disease, dementia, multiple sclerosis, or other neurological disorder can be difficult, and in most cases, is a long-term and often full-time job. . . .

There are hundreds of neurological disorders, each with disease-specific symptoms and a different progression. The first step in caring for someone with a neurological disease is learning as much as you can about the illness in general, and working with your healthcare provider to understand the possible course the disease will take for your loved one. Multiple resources are available for gathering information about neurological disorders, including healthcare providers, librarians, nongovernmental organizations or non-profits; many online resources can provide useful information for you and your loved one. . . .

About Alzheimer's Disease

Alzheimer s disease (AD) is the most common form of dementia, a term used to describe a group of symptoms affecting intellectual and social abilities severely enough to interfere with daily functioning. Memory loss generally occurs in dementia, but memory loss alone doesn't mean you have dementia. Dementia indicates problems with at least two brain functions, such as memory loss along with impaired judgment on language. Dementia

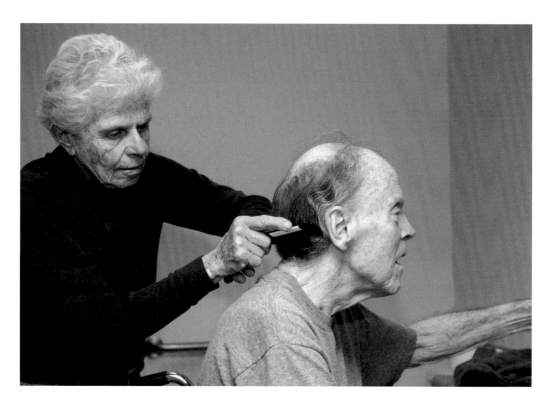

can cause confusion and an inability to remember people and names.

Dementia may also cause changes in personality and social behavior. The second most common form of dementia is called vascular dementia, which is an umbrella term used to describe a series of conditions caused by problems in the supply of blood to the brain, often as a result of stroke(s) or small [blood] vessel disease.

Alzheimer's disease occurs in one in ten people over the age of 65. According to recent assessments, the rate of Alzheimer's disease is going to nearly double every 20 years. By 2050, 43 percent of those with Alzheimer's disease will need high-level care, equivalent to that of a nursing home. The largest increase in the prevalence will occur in Asia, where the number of Alzheimer's cases is expected to grow from 12.65 million in 2006 to 62.85 million in 2050.

Caring for someone with a neurogenerative disorder can be a difficult and often long-term, full-time job. (© David Young-Wolff/ Alamy)

Alzheimer's disease is often thought about in three stages:

- *Mild Alzheimer's disease* (also called early-stage). In mild AD, the first stage, people often have some memory loss and small changes in their personality. They may have trouble remembering recent events or the names of familiar people or things. They may no longer be able to solve simple math problems or balance a checkbook. People with mild AD also slowly lose the ability to plan and organise. For example, they may have trouble making a grocery list and finding items in the store.
- *Moderate Alzheimer's disease.* This is the middle stage of AD. Memory loss and confusion become more obvious. People have more trouble organizing, planning and following instructions. They may need help getting dressed and may start having problems with incontinence. This means they can't control their bladder and/or bowels. People with moderate-stage AD may have trouble recognizing family members and friends. They may not know where they are or what day or year it is. They also may lack judgment and begin to wander, so people with moderate AD should not be left alone. They may become restless and begin repeating movements late in the day. Also, they may have trouble sleeping. Personality changes can become more serious. People with moderate AD may make threats, accuse others of stealing, curse, kick, hit, bite, scream or grab things.

About Multiple Sclerosis

Researchers believe multiple sclerosis (MS) is an autoimmune disease of the central nervous system where communication between the brain and other parts of the body is disrupted due to a break down in the insulating myelin that surrounds a person's nerves. The manifestation of this disease for each individual is different, depending upon where the damage occurs in the individual's central nervous system, and how extensive the damage is.

Common symptoms include fatigue, weakness of arms and legs, numbness, lack of coordination, loss of balance, visual problems, loss of bladder or bowel control, depression and emotional changes, cognitive problems and difficulty speaking. MS is not contagious or fatal, but a small number of people have a severe type of MS that may shorten life expectancy.

Today over 2,000,000 people around the world have MS. Women are more likely to develop MS than men. There are four commonly-discussed disease courses for MS. For those newly diagnosed, it may not be clear what type you have for some time.

> **FAST FACT**
>
> According to the National Family Caregivers Association, during any given year more than 65 million people—29 percent of the US population—provide an estimated $375 billion worth of free care for a chronically ill, disabled, or aged family member or friend, and 1.4 million children aged eight to eighteen care for an adult relative.

- *Relapsing/Remitting.* The majority of people diagnosed with MS—approximately 90%—are diagnosed with the relapsing/remitting type. The symptoms affect most people in their early 20s, after which there are periodic attacks (relapses), followed by partial or complete recovery (remissions). A relapse can last for a few days to several months. The severity can also vary. Symptoms may remain after relapse due to nerve damage. The pattern of nerves affected, severity of attacks, degree of recovery, and time between relapses all vary widely from person to person. Eventually, most people with relapsing/remitting MS will enter a secondary progressive phase of MS.
- *Secondary Progressive.* People with this type of MS may have started with a diagnosis of relapsing/remitting and then started to experience a worsening

of symptoms over many years. In this type of MS, the course of symptoms steadily [progresses], without relapses or remissions. The transition typically occurs between 10 and 20 years after the diagnosis of relapsing/remitting MS. Progression occurs at a different rate in each person and generally leads to some disability.

• *Primary Progressive.* In this form of MS, the disease begins with a slow progression of neurological deficits where symptoms appear and gradually worsen over time, without significant plateaus or remissions. A person with primary progressive MS, by definition, does not experience acute attacks.

• *Progressive Relapsing.* Progressive relapsing MS is the least common form of disease—approximately 5 percent of people with MS have this form. Relapses or attacks occur periodically. However, symptoms continue and are progressive in between relapses.

The above list represents very broad categories for MS. It does not definitively or adequately describe the experiences *everyone* has with the disease. It is difficult to predict who will remain relatively stable over time and who will progress or how quickly. The final stages of MS vary greatly for each individual with the disease, although most will see an increase in symptoms.

About Other Neurological Disorders

There are literally hundreds of neurological disorders that require care at various stages and different care as they each progress. If you or someone you know is a caregiver for a loved one with a neurological disorder, the first step is to find out as much as you can about the disease and its course. The next step is to connect with people who are involved in caring for individuals with the disease. There are multiple caregiving support groups across the world,

Some of the Neurodegenerative Disorders

This list includes some of the most common or most frequently mentioned neurodegenerative diseases. Available estimates of their prevalence vary widely because different studies use different methods of estimation and because many people with these disorders have not been diagnosed. The starred disorders are inherited.

Disease	Estimate
Alzheimer's disease	13% of people over 65
Amyotrophic lateral sclerosis (Lou Gehrig's disease)	5.2 per 100,000
Charcot-Marie-Tooth disorder*	32.5 per 100,000
Corticobasal degeneration	4 per 100,000
Creutzfeldt-Jakob disease (human form of mad cow disease)	0.1 per 100,00
Fatal family insomnia*	Extremely rare
Friedreich's ataxia*	2 per 100,000
Frontotemporal dementia (Pick's disease)	3 per 100,000
Frontotemporal lobar degeneration	9 to 15 per 100,000
Huntington's disease*	7 per 100,000
Kennedy disease*	3.3 per 100,000
Lewy body dementia	1.3 million in U.S.
Multiple sclerosis	91.7 per 100,000
Multiple system atrophy	4.6 per 100,000
Niemann-Pick disease*	2.5 per 100,000
Parkinson's disease	100 to 300 per 100,000
Progressive aphasia	2.5 per 100,000
Progressive supranuclear palsy	6 per 100,000
Sanfilippo Syndrome*	0.3 per 100,000
Tay-Sachs disease*	0.3 per 100,000

as well as disease-specific support and advocacy organizations that have caregiver information and/or support available. Talk to your healthcare provider or go to your local health agency or library, or search online for relevant resources and support.

Caring for someone with a neurological disorder can be a rewarding experience, but it can also have a significant impact on a caregiver's own life and health, both physical and emotional. Taking an educated and balanced approach to this important work will serve you and your loved one best over the course of the illness. Seeking input and support from friends and others who have done this work can prove invaluable, and lessen the stress or anxiety you might feel from not knowing what to expect.

For most neurological disorders, recognizing the ever-changing nature of the illness is a critical first step. Very often, the path will be unpredictable or will appear to be heading in one direction, only to suddenly change. As a caregiver, learning to accept these uncertainties may be the most difficult part of your work—and is very stressful, in and of itself. At the same time, making future plans is also important. This may seem counter-intuitive, as it is hard to plan when you don't know what to expect, but there are many parts of caregiving that can be predicted, such as planning for regular doctor's appointments and daily routines such as mealtimes and other care. Learning all you can about the disease provides an anchor as the disease course begins to unfold.

Parkinson's Disease Causes Declining Ability to Control Movement

Parkinson's Disease Foundation

Parkinson's disease (PD) is a neurodegenerative disorder that affects movement, producing symptoms such as tremor of the hands, arms, legs, and face; slowness of movement; stiffness of the limbs; and impaired balance. It results from the death of neurons in the brain that produce dopamine, a chemical involved in the control of movement and coordination, but why these neurons die is unknown. The disease affects different individuals differently, progressing slowly in some and rapidly in others, and sometimes starts on only one side of the body. PD is not fatal, but it cannot be cured, although scientists are working toward an understanding of its cause that may lead to a cure in the future. So far, the available treatments merely help to manage the symptoms.

The Parkinson's Disease Foundation funds research and supports people living with PD through a variety of programs and services.

Parkinson's disease (PD) is chronic and progressive movement disorder, meaning that symptoms continue and worsen over time. Nearly one million people in the US are living with Parkinson's disease. The cause is unknown, and although there is presently no cure, there are treatment options such as medication and surgery to manage its symptoms.

Parkinson's involves the malfunction and death of vital nerve cells in the brain, called neurons. Parkinson's primarily affects neurons in the area of the brain called the substantia nigra. Some of these dying neurons produce dopamine, a chemical that sends messages to the part of the brain that controls movement and coordination. As PD progresses, the amount of dopamine produced in the brain decreases, leaving a person unable to control movement normally.

The specific group of symptoms that an individual experiences varies from person to person. Primary motor signs of Parkinson's disease include the following.

- *tremor* of the hands, arms, legs, jaw and face
- *bradykinesia* or slowness of movement
- *rigidity* or stiffness of the limbs and trunk
- *postural instability* or impaired balance and coordination

Scientists are also exploring the idea that loss of cells in other areas of the brain and body contribute to Parkinson's. For example, researchers have discovered that the hallmark sign of Parkinson's disease—clumps of a protein alpha-synuclein, which are also called Lewy Bodies—are found not only in the mid-brain but also in the brain stem and the olfactory bulb.

These areas of the brain correlate to nonmotor functions such as sense of smell and sleep regulation. The presence of Lewy bodies in these areas could explain the nonmotor symptoms experienced by some people with PD before any motor sign of the disease appears. The intestines also have dopamine cells that degenerate in Parkinson's, and this may be important in the gastrointestinal symptoms that are part of the disease.

Symptoms

The diagnosis of PD depends upon the presence of one or more of the four most common motor symptoms of the disease. In addition, there are other secondary and nonmotor symptoms that affect many people and are increasingly recognized by doctors as important to treating Parkinson's.

Each person with Parkinson's will experience symptoms differently. For example, many people experience tremor as their primary symptom, while others may not have tremors, but may have problems with balance. Also, for some people the disease progresses quickly, and in others it does not.

By definition, Parkinson's is a progressive disease. Although some people with Parkinson's only have symptoms on one side of the body for many years, eventually the symptoms begin on the other side. Symptoms on the other side of the body often do not become as severe as symptoms on the initial side.

Who Has Parkinson's?

- As many as one million Americans live with Parkinson's disease, which is more than the combined number of people diagnosed with multiple sclerosis, muscular dystrophy and Lou Gehrig's disease.
- Approximately 60,000 Americans are diagnosed with Parkinson's disease each year, and this number does not reflect the thousands of cases that go undetected.
- An estimated seven to 10 million people worldwide are living with Parkinson's disease.
- Incidence of Parkinson's increases with age, but an estimated four percent of people with PD are diagnosed before the age of 50.
- Men are one and a half times more likely to have Parkinson's than women. . . .

Causes

To date, despite decades of intensive study, the causes of Parkinson's remain unknown. Many experts think that the disease is caused by a combination of genetic and environmental factors, which may vary from person to person.

In some people, genetic factors may play a role; in others, illness, an environmental toxin or other event may contribute to PD. Scientists have identified aging as an important risk factor; there is a two to four percent risk for Parkinson's among people over age 60, compared with one to two percent in the general population.

The chemical or genetic trigger that starts the cell death process in dopamine neurons is the subject of intense scientific study. Many believe that by understanding the sequence of events that leads to the loss of dopamine cells, scientists will be able to develop treatments to stop or reverse the disease.

A Parkinson's patient undergoes an examination in a doctor's office. Primary Parkinson's signs include tremors, slowness of movement, rigidity or stiffness of the limbs and trunk, and impaired balance and coordination. (© Aurora Photos/Alamy)

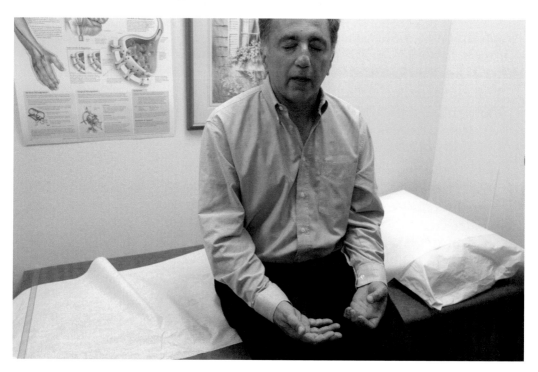

The vast majority of Parkinson's cases are not directly inherited. About 15 to 25 percent of people with Parkinson's report having a relative with the disease. In large population studies, researchers have found that people with an affected first-degree relative, such as a parent or sibling, have a four to nine percent higher chance of developing PD, as compared to the general population. This means that if a person's parent has PD, his or her chances of developing the disease are slightly higher than the risk among the general population. . . .

Progression

The progression of Parkinson's disease varies among different individuals. Parkinson's is chronic and slowly progressive, meaning that symptoms continue and worsen over a period of years. Parkinson's is not considered a fatal disease. And the way that it progresses it different for everyone:

- Movement symptoms vary from person to person, and so does the rate at which they progress.
- Some are more bothersome than others depending on what a person normally does during the day.
- Some people with Parkinson's live with mild symptoms for many years, whereas others develop movement difficulties more quickly.
- Nonmotor symptoms also are very individualized, and they affect most people with Parkinson's at all stages of disease. Some people with Parkinson's find that symptoms such as depression or fatigue interfere more with daily life than do problems with movement. . . .

Chasing the Cure

Many scientists believe that the cure for Parkinson's will come from a deeper understanding of what causes the disease. What is the reason that dopamine neurons begin to degenerate and die?

If the cause of the neurodegeneration can be identified, perhaps a specific treatment can be developed to slow, stop or reverse its process. Future treatment strategies may include the delivery of substances or genetic material directly to the brain. They may involve replacing neurons.

However, these techniques are in the earliest stages of development. For people living with Parkinson's disease and their families, the progress is always too slow. But there are reasons to be optimistic. It is anticipated that many scientific advances will be translated into benefits for people with Parkinson's, and so the hope for a cure is linked with true promise and great optimism.

ALS Causes Muscle Weakness and Loss of Ability to Swallow or Speak

Les Turner Foundation

Amyotrophic lateral sclerosis (ALS, also called Lou Gehrig's disease,) is a neurodegenerative disease that affects motor neurons, the nerve cells in the brain that control the body's muscles. When the motor neurons stop functioning, the muscles waste away, causing progressively worsening weakness and twitching of the limbs. There can also be difficulty in speaking or swallowing. There is no specific test for ALS, so a diagnosis can be made only by ruling out other conditions, including several other neurodegenerative diseases that are similar. ALS progresses at different rates in each individual, but is incurable and always fatal, often within three to five years. Treatment consists of therapy and medications that help to manage the symptoms, but the patient eventually becomes a full-time responsibility for his or her caregivers.

The Les Turner Foundation provides medical care to ALS patients in the Chicago area and is one of the nation's largest independent organizations that raises funds to fight ALS.

ALS—often referred to as Lou Gehrig's disease or motor neuron disease (MND)—is a progressive, degenerative disease affecting motor neurons. Motor neurons are specialized nerve cells that carry impulses from the brain to the muscles by way of the brainstem and the spinal cord. The muscles then move in response to these impulses.

In ALS, motor neurons gradually cease functioning and die. As this happens, the muscle tissues waste away because no movement is being stimulated. This results in gradually worsening muscle weakness, atrophy, and often spasticity. Only the motor neurons are affected. Other nerve cells, such as sensory neurons that bring information from sense organs to the brain, remain healthy.

ALS occurs throughout the world regardless of race, ethnicity or socioeconomic status. Men are affected slightly more frequently than women. It most commonly occurs between 40 and 70 years of age, although the disease can strike at any age.

More than 5,600 Americans are diagnosed with ALS each year. Approximately 35,000 people at any given time are living with ALS in the United States. The incidence of ALS is close to that of multiple sclerosis and four times that of muscular dystrophy.

What Are the Symptoms of ALS?

Some of the early symptoms of ALS might include:

- Weakness or poor coordination in one limb
- Changes in speaking or swallowing
- Unusual muscle twitches, spasms, or cramps
- Unusual weight loss or loss of muscle bulk

Typically, ALS affects motor neurons in both the brainstem and spinal cord. Symptoms related to the brainstem neurons (sometimes referred to as "bulbar symptoms") can include spasticity or stiffness in the lower limbs, face, or jaw. Feelings of heaviness, fatigue,

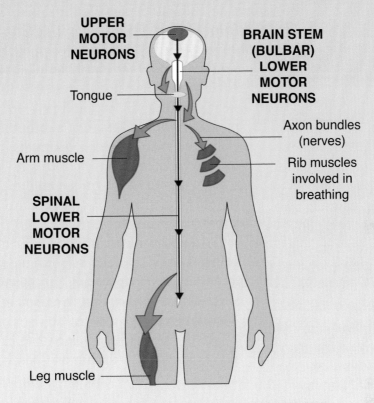

Muscles Affected by ALS

UPPER MOTOR NEURONS

BRAIN STEM (BULBAR) LOWER MOTOR NEURONS

Tongue

Axon bundles (nerves)

Arm muscle

Rib muscles involved in breathing

SPINAL LOWER MOTOR NEURONS

Leg muscle

Taken from: Muscular Dystrophy Association. *Facts About Amyotrophic Lateral Sclerosis*, April 2011. www.als-mda.org/publications/PDF/FA-ALS.pdf.

stiffness, and lack of coordination are common. Reflexes may be very brisk, or exaggerated.

Unprovoked outbursts of laughter or crying can occur, a condition often referred to as "pseudobulbar affect" or "emotional lability." Symptoms related to the spinal cord neurons (sometimes referred to as "somatic symptoms") can include weakness, muscle wasting, or muscle twitching.

It is important to remember that ALS strikes people in different ways. The symptoms and progression of the disease will be different from person to person.

The diagnosis of ALS is a "clinical diagnosis," meaning there is no specific test for it. Often, tests will be administered to rule out illnesses with similar symptoms. These may include an MRI of the brain or spinal cord, an electromyography (EMG) study of nerve and muscle function, and a variety of blood and urine tests. After reviewing these test results and the patient's medical history, and performing a complete neurological exam, a neuromuscular specialist can usually reach a diagnosis. It may take several months of observation and retesting to reach a definitive diagnosis, and that diagnosis should be confirmed via a second opinion from another neuromuscular specialist.

ALS progresses at different rates in each individual. The average survival for someone affected by ALS is three to five years. Fifty percent of those affected pass away within five years of diagnosis. A small percentage may live 10 years or more.

As the disease progresses, the patient usually experiences a decline in speech, swallowing, and limb strength and function. Generally, ALS is not a physically painful condition, though discomfort can result from immobility and muscle shortening. The ALS patient usually remains alert and retains normal sensation, vision, bowel and bladder function. While most patients do not have loss of intellectual function, some may have subtle changes in mood, behavior, or personality. In a small minority of patients, more significant changes in behavior and judgment suggest a form of dementia.

What Causes ALS?

Approximately 10 percent of all ALS cases are inherited forms, known as "familial ALS. Several genes have been identified that cause familial ALS. The remaining 90 percent of cases are called "sporadic ALS."

FAST FACT

In the United States ALS is often called Lou Gehrig's disease because it became known to the American public when Lou Gehrig, a star baseball player for the New York Yankees in the 1920s and 1930s, publicly announced that he had to retire from playing baseball due to the disease. He died two years later.

In 2011, researchers, . . . identified a common cause of all forms of ALS: a broken-down protein "recycling system" in the neurons of the spinal cord and brain. Additional research is needed to determine how best to treat this faulty pathway.

Many of the symptoms of ALS are treatable, but there are no drugs or treatments to cure the disease. However, patients may elect to take Rilutek, the first FDA-approved medication for the treatment of ALS, as it has been shown to modestly increase lifespan. In addition, Nuedexta is approved by the FDA [Food and Drug Administration] to treat pseudobulbar affect, a symptom that can occur in ALS/MND and other neurological conditions. Decisions regarding medication should be made in consultation with a neuromuscular specialist and should be part of a comprehensive treatment approach.

ALS progresses at a different rate in each individual victim of the disease, but the average survival rate is three to five years. (© ZUMA Wire Service/ Alamy)

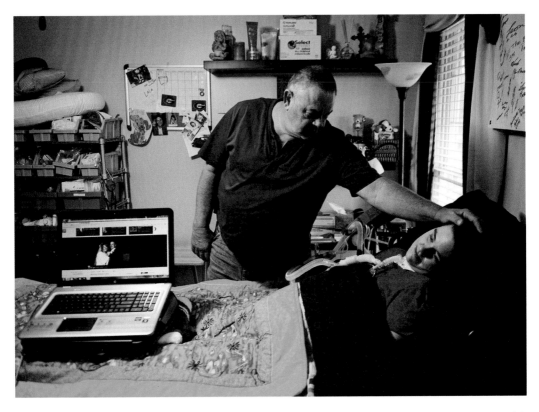

The quality of life of patients with ALS can often be improved by various treatments and interventions. Care provided by experts in multidisciplinary centers has been shown to prolong survival. Proper positioning, exercise, physical therapy, and medications can help patients manage their symptoms. A feeding tube may be suggested if there is inadequate nutrition, extended meal times, rapid weight loss, high risk of aspiration (inhaling food or liquids into the lungs), or recurrent pneumonia. A wide range of devices and techniques can address problems with communication. Ultimately, ALS may result in sleep interruptions and changes in breathing, requiring consideration of airway clearance therapies. This may range from medications to non-invasive (mask) ventilation to a tracheostomy [a breathing tube surgically inserted into the throat] with mechanical ventilation. Managing symptoms is often a full-time responsibility for the patient and their caregivers. . . .

ALS is the most serious disease among several that affect motor neurons. Other diseases in this group, called motor neuron diseases (MND), include spinal muscular atrophy (SMA), primary lateral sclerosis (PLS) and spinal bulbar muscular atrophy (Kennedy's Disease). Only a comprehensive examination by a neurologist can determine whether symptoms are caused by ALS or one of these other conditions.

Huntington's Disease Causes Abnormal Movement, Thinking, and Behavior

Gale Encyclopedia of Medicine

The following viewpoint from the *Gale Encyclopedia of Medicine* explains that Huntington's (or Huntington) disease (HD) is an inherited neurodegenerative disease that causes uncontrolled physical movement and progressive mental deterioration. It used to be called Huntington's chorea, which means "dance," because it is characterized by involuntary movement of the feet and arms. A person with a parent who has the disease has a 50 percent chance of inheriting the HD gene. Onset of the disease occurs usually between the ages of thirty and fifty, although in some cases it can begin in childhood or early adolescence. Its physical and mental symptoms vary from person to person but generally become severe enough to impair daily functioning, resulting in the eventual need for a caregiver. Treatment can help with management of symptoms, but death usually occurs between ten and thirty years after onset. Experiments are under way on new treatments that show promise.

Huntington disease (HD) is a progressive neurodegenerative disease causing uncontrolled physical movements and mental deterioration. The disease was discovered by George Sumner Huntington (1850–1916), an Ohio doctor who first described the hereditary movement disorder in 1872.

Huntington disease is also called Huntington chorea or hereditary chorea. The word *chorea* comes from the Greek word for "dance" and refers to the involuntary movements of the patient's feet, lower arms, and face that develop as the disease progresses. It is occasionally referred to as "Woody Guthrie's disease" for the American folk singer who died from it. Huntington disease (HD) causes progressive loss of cells in areas of the brain responsible for certain aspects of movement control and mental abilities. A person with HD gradually develops abnormal movements and changes in cognition (thinking), behavior and personality.

The onset of symptoms of HD usually occurs between the ages of 30 and 50; although in 10 percent of cases, onset is in late childhood or early adolescence. Approximately 30,000 people in the United States are affected by HD, with another 150,000 at risk for developing this disorder. The frequency of HD is 4–7 cases per 100,000 persons.

Causes and Symptoms

Huntington disease is caused by a defect in the HD gene (an inherited unit which contains a code for a protein), which is located on the short arm of chromosome 4. The gene codes for a protein called huntingtin, whose function is not known as of early [2012]. The nucleotide codes (building blocks of genes arranged in a specific code which chemically forms into proteins), contain CAG [a nucleotide of cytosine, adenine, and guanine] repeats (40 or more of these repeat sequences). The extra building blocks in the huntingtin gene cause the protein that is made from it to contain an extra section as well. It is currently thought that this extra protein section, or portion, interacts with other proteins in brain cells where it occurs, and that this interaction ultimately leads to cell death.

The HD gene is a dominant gene, meaning that only one copy of it is needed to develop the disease. HD affects both males and females. The gene may be inherited from either parent, who will also be affected by the disease. A parent with the HD gene has a 50 percent chance of passing it onto each offspring. The chances of passing on the HD gene are not affected by the results of previous pregnancies.

The symptoms of HD fall into three categories: motor or movement symptoms; personality and behavioral changes; and cognitive decline. The severity and rate of progression of each type of symptom can vary from person to person.

Early motor symptoms include restlessness, twitching and a desire to move about. Handwriting may become less controlled, and coordination may decline. Later symptoms include:

- dystonia, or sustained abnormal postures, including facial grimaces, a twisted neck, or an arched back
- chorea, in which involuntary jerking, twisting or writhing motions become pronounced
- slowness of voluntary movements, inability to regulate the speed or force of movements, inability to initiate movement and slowed reactions
- difficulty speaking and swallowing due to involvement of the throat muscles
- localized or generalized weakness and impaired balance ability
- rigidity, especially in late-stage disease

Personality and behavioral changes include depression, irritability, anxiety and apathy. The person with HD may become impulsive, aggressive or socially withdrawn.

Cognitive changes include loss of ability to plan and execute routine tasks, slowed thought, and impaired or inappropriate judgment. Short-term memory loss usually occurs, although long-term memory is usually not affected. The person with late-stage HD usually retains knowledge of his environment and recognizes family members or other loved ones, despite severe cognitive decline.

Diagnosis

Diagnosis of HD begins with a detailed medical history, and a thorough physical and neurological examination. The family's medical history is very important. Magnetic resonance imaging (MRI) or computed tomography scan (CT scan) imaging may be performed to look for degeneration in the basal ganglia and cortex, the brain regions most affected in HD.

Physicians have recently developed a Uniform Huntington's Disease Rating Scale, or UHDRS, to assess a patient's symptoms and the speed of progression of the disease.

A genetic test is available for confirmation of the clinical diagnosis. In this test, a small blood sample is taken, and DNA from it is analyzed to determine the CAG repeat number. A person with a repeat number of 30 or below will not develop HD. A person with a repeat number between 35 and 40 may not develop the disease within their normal lifespan. A person with a very high number of repeats (70 or above) is likely to develop the juvenile-onset form. An important part of genetic testing is extensive genetic counseling.

Prenatal testing is available. A person at risk for HD (a child of an affected person) may obtain fetal testing without determining whether she herself carries the gene. This test, also called a linkage test, examines the pattern of DNA near the gene in both parent and fetus, but does not analyze for the triple nucleotide repeat (CAG). If the

DNA patterns do not match, the fetus can be assumed not to have inherited the HD gene, even if present in the parent. A pattern match indicates the fetus probably has the same genetic makeup of the at-risk parent.

Treatment

There is no cure for HD, nor any treatment that can slow the rate of progression. Treatment is aimed at reducing the disability caused by the motor impairments, and treating behavioral and emotional symptoms.

Physical therapy is used to maintain strength and compensate for lost strength and balance. Stretching and range of motion exercises help minimize contracture, or muscle shortening, a result of weakness and disuse. The physical therapist also advises on the use of mobility aids such as walkers or wheelchairs.

Motor symptoms may be treated with drugs, although some studies suggest that anti-chorea treatment rarely improves function. . . .

Occupational therapy is used to design compensatory strategies for lost abilities in the activities of daily living, such as eating, dressing, and grooming. The occupational therapist advises on modifications to the home that improve safety, accessibility, and comfort.

Difficulty swallowing may be lessened by preparation of softer foods, blending food in an electric blender, and taking care to eat slowly and carefully. Use of a straw for all liquids can help. The potential for choking on food is a concern, especially late in the disease progression. . . . In addition, passage of food into the airways increases the risk for pneumonia. A gastric feeding tube may be needed, if swallowing becomes too difficult or dangerous.

Speech difficulties may be partially compensated by using picture boards or other augmentative communication

> **FAST FACT**
>
> A person who inherits the HD gene will eventually get the disease unless he or she dies of something else before symptoms develop. Research has shown that at-risk adults who inherit the gene without having been warned by their parents are often angry and resentful because they were not given a chance to plan ahead.

Huntington's disease causes a progressive loss of cells in areas of the brain responsible for certain aspects of movement control and mental abilities. (© Conor Caffrey/Photo Researchers, Inc.)

devices. Loss of cognitive ability affects both speech production and understanding. A speech-language pathologist can work with the family to develop simplified and more directed communication strategies, including speaking slowly, using simple words, and repeating sentences exactly.

Early behavioral changes, including depression and anxiety, may respond to drug therapy. Maintaining a calm, familiar, and secure environment is useful as the disease progresses. Support groups for both patients and caregivers form an important part of treatment.

Additional Treatments

Experimental transplant of fetal brain tissue has been attempted in a few HD patients. Early results show some promise, but further trials are needed to establish the effectiveness of this treatment. . . .

In 2004 the Food and Drug Administration (FDA) also approved deep brain stimulation (DBS) as an acceptable treatment for HD and other movement disorders. In DBS, the surgeon implants a battery-operated medical device called a neurostimulator, which delivers electrical impulses to the areas of the brain that govern movement. . . .

Psychotherapy is often recommended for individuals who know themselves to be at risk for the disease. Some persons want to know their risk status while others prefer not to be tested. Psychotherapy may be useful in helping at-risk persons decide about testing as well as coping with the results of the test.

The person with Huntington disease may be able to maintain a job for several years after diagnosis, despite the increase in disability. Loss of cognitive functions and increase in motor and behavioral symptoms eventually prevent the person with HD from continuing employment. Ultimately, severe motor symptoms prevent mobility. Death usually occurs between 10 and 30 years after disease onset, typically as the result of pneumonia or a fall. Progressive weakness of respiratory and swallowing muscles leads to increased risk of respiratory infection and choking, the most common causes of death. Future research in this area is currently focusing on nerve cell transplantation.

Multiple Sclerosis Is a Disabling Disorder That Sometimes Develops Slowly

MS Watch

Although in the past multiple sclerosis (MS) was thought to be a strictly inflammatory disease of the central nervous system (CNS), caused by some unknown factor that triggers the body's immune system, it is now believed that the nerve damage it involves may begin before the inflammation. Recently, therefore, it has come to be considered a neurodegenerative disease. The inflammation of nerves in the CNS produces damage to their myelin sheaths, resulting in symptoms that generally go away temporarily as the sheaths are repaired, but eventually the damage extends to the underlying nerve fibers—and in fact, the neurodegeneration appears to be independent of the inflammatory sheath damage. Its underlying cause is unknown, but researchers hope to develop treatments that can prevent or at least retard its progression.

MS Watch is a Canadian website providing information about multiple sclerosis.

MS was once considered to be strictly an inflammatory disease of the central nervous system (CNS; the brain and spinal cord). During an MS relapse, a flare-up in the body's immune system causes inflammation and swelling in the CNS. For example, inflammation of the optic nerve (leading to the eye) can cause vision problems and eye pain, a condition known as optic neuritis. Inflammation of the sensory or motor nerves can produce sensory symptoms, such as tingling or numbness, or motor (i.e. muscle) symptoms, such as weakness or spasms. As the inflammatory flare-up subsides, these symptoms tend to go away (or "remit") either completely or partially. This is why the most common form of MS is called relapsing-remitting MS: episodes of relapses are followed by periods of remission.

What triggers these inflammatory flare-ups? That mystery still hasn't been solved but a number of key factors appear to be involved. There may be an initial trigger, such as a virus or some other toxic factor, which "turns on" the immune system, although a specific trigger has not been isolated.

Once the immune system is activated in people with MS, there are two key problems. Activated cells of the immune system migrate from the body into the CNS across what is known as the blood-brain barrier (BBB), a physical barrier of tightly-packed cells that is there to screen out injurious substances from entering the brain. Once inside the CNS, these activated immune cells, called T cells, attack the body's own tissues. This is why MS is believed to be an autoimmune disorder.

The second problem is that once the attack gets underway, it doesn't switch off as it should. Normally, when the immune system detects a foreign invader, such as a virus or a bacterium, it signals a red alert and attacks it with its arsenal of weapons. Once the invader has been killed or inactivated, the immune system shuts down the attack and goes back to its role of patrolling the body.

In MS, the inflammatory response persists. Prolonged inflammation is very injurious to the delicate nerve fibres (or axons) in the CNS. Immune cells can damage the nerves' protective covering, called myelin. Immune cells can directly attack the myelin, or they can release toxic chemicals that erode it. Either way, the myelin begins to deteriorate, a process called demyelination. Just as damaged insulation can cause a wire to short-circuit, damaged myelin disrupts the messages traveling along the nerve fibers. The "short-circuits" are experienced as MS symptoms, such as tingling, numbness or pain. . . .

Nerve Degeneration

Inflammatory lesions in the CNS can cause significant damage to the myelin sheath (called demyelination), which protects nerve fibres (axons), as well as to the nerves themselves. The deterioration in myelin can be repaired, although this in-built repair mechanism appears to become less effective after repeated inflammatory relapses.

More serious, however, is the damage that can be caused to the underlying nerve fibres. It is this nerve damage that is believed to result in permanent neurological deficits and disability. Numerous studies have shown that significant nerve damage occurs within active MS lesions in the CNS as a result of the effects of inflammation. During an inflammatory flare-up, many chemicals (e.g. cytokines and enzymes that degrade proteins) are released that are toxic to nerves. It is believed that this can ultimately lead to axonal transection, i.e. the severing of the nerve fibre. Axonal damage and transection can occur even in people who have had MS for only a short time.

It might be supposed that as the insulating myelin is stripped away, there would be a corresponding loss of the nerve "wiring". However, the precise relationship between the loss of myelin and the loss of axons has not been fully worked out. In general, axonal loss is related to the amount of inflammatory activity in MS lesions, but damage can still occur in older, inactive lesions as well as in recovering lesions that are undergoing remyelination.

This suggests that neurodegeneration is an ongoing process that is somewhat independent of inflammation. Indeed, recent research has suggested that neurodegeneration begins early in the MS disease course—even before inflammation is apparent—and continues thereafter. If you imagine that MS is a forest fire, inflammation is the match that will cause the most visible flare-ups. But before the match is struck, the undergrowth may already be smouldering. Neurodegeneration is that slow burn, which will continue to smoulder long after the forest fire of inflammation has been suppressed. This would explain why strictly anti-inflammatory medications, such as steroids, do not affect the longer term process of nerve degeneration: the inflammatory flare-up is doused, but the slow burn of neurodegeneration continues. Similarly, in progressive forms of deterioration, the neurodegenerative process is rapid and severe even when there is little or no significant inflammation. No match is lit, but the forest still burns.

FAST FACT

Multiple sclerosis is most commonly diagnosed in people between the ages of twenty and forty. It affects more women than men. How rapidly it progresses varies, but many patients can continue to walk and function at work for at least twenty years.

Ideally, a treatment would prevent this process of axonal damage. But why are axons so important? Many researchers believe that axonal loss is the principal determinant of disability. For example, one small autopsy study of five people with severely disabling MS found that in their chronic brain lesions, about two-thirds of the axons had been lost compared to people without MS. These individuals' disabilities appeared to be due largely to this extensive loss of nerve cells in their brains.

How Is Neurodegeneration Measured?

Researchers use a number of tools to try and assess the extent of neurodegeneration that occurs in MS. The most direct way is to examine MS lesions at autopsy after a person has passed away. New research techniques, such as magnetic resonance spectroscopy (MRS), provide a less invasive approach (and can be done while people are still alive). MRS involves imaging the brain and spinal cord to identify the presence of certain chemicals that indicate nerve damage. Of particular interest is a substance called NAA (N-acetyl aspartate), an amino acid that is fairly specific to neurons and axons; it is rarely found outside of nerves. The level of NAA has been shown to be lower in MS lesions, notably in chronic T1 lesions (called "chronic black holes"). This indicates that there is a lower density of nerve cells, presumably because of neurodegeneration. Older MS lesions also show substantial loss of axons, as assessed by NAA levels. In addition, MRS studies have shown that there is diffuse injury to axons early in MS—even before there is any sign of disability.

A more global measure of tissue change is brain atrophy, or shrinkage. MRI can provide a good estimate of the total amount of tissue in the brain. Studies have shown that the amount of tissue in everyone's brain declines with aging. However, this brain atrophy progresses faster in people with MS versus those without MS. Compared with other MRI metrics, the extent of brain atrophy is well correlated with clinical disability. There are several possible causes of brain atrophy in MS, including loss of myelin (demyelination) and axons. However, atrophy measures can be influenced by many things. Steroid treatments, for example, actually decrease the volume of the brain because they reduce swelling. Similarly, neurodegeneration can reduce atrophy in some cases because it may lead to overproduction of other cells.

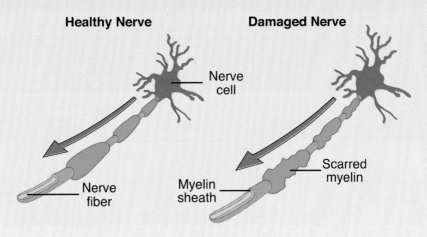

Nerve Damage in Multiple Sclerosis

In multiple sclerosis, the myelin sheaths of the nerve fibers that connect nerve cells are damaged by scars.

Healthy Nerve

Damaged Nerve

Nerve cell

Nerve fiber

Myelin sheath

Scarred myelin

Taken from: Mayor's Health Line Blog (Boston), March 28, 2011. http://mayorshealthline.wordpress.com/2011/03/28/a-better-understanding-of-multiple-sclerosis-ms/.

MS Disease Progression

During the course of MS, inflammation and neurode-generation cause a significant amount of axonal loss. But this loss of axons does not necessarily result in per-manent deficits or disabilities—at least not right away. There are several reasons for this. Lesions may appear in what are known as "clinically silent" areas. This means that the brain region affected is not directly tied to a type of function. In contrast, damage to certain parts of the nervous system, such as the optic nerve, is more likely to produce symptoms right away.

Secondly, the brain is able to adapt to the loss of tis-sue by shifting the work of those lost axons to other nerve cells. The responsibility for a given task may be moved to adjoining brain regions, or even to a region on the op-posite side of the brain. A "left-brain" task may become a "right-brain" task, and vice-versa. This ability to adapt how functions are performed is called brain plasticity.

While the brain can compensate for some degree of injury, it loses some of this ability as time passes. Brain plasticity appears to decline with time in everyone, not just people with MS. In addition, as the brain experiences repeated injuries caused by relapse after relapse, its capacity to repair and adapt may become exhausted. In other words, the slow accumulation of damage reaches a "tipping point": once a certain threshold of tissue loss

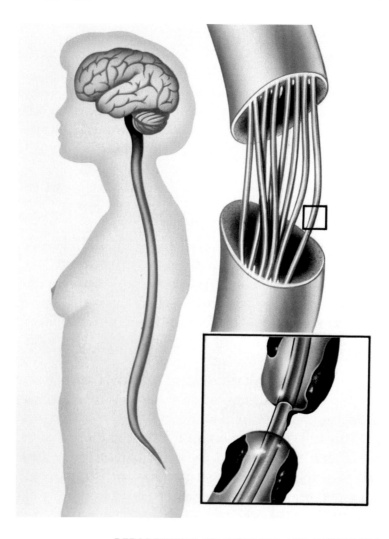

This illustration of a woman with multiple sclerosis shows a magnified view of the spinal cord with individual nerve fibers; at lower right is a magnified view of the nerve fibers' axons, in which the myelin sheaths have been destroyed by MS.
(© John Bavosi/Photo Researchers, Inc.)

has been reached, the cumulative effect results in permanent neurological deficits that begin to progress thereafter. The effect is not unlike an avalanche: snow gradually builds up until there is one snowflake too many, and the whole mass begins to fall.

This may be what occurs in secondary-progressive MS. During the relapsing-remitting phase of the disease, damage slowly accumulates over many years. Then a critical point is reached, and the progressive phase begins. Thereafter, the development of disability is much more rapid than during the relapsing-remitting phase.

One large study of an MS population found that there was a very wide variation in the amount of time it took for people to develop moderate disability. . . . Some people reached that point within a year of diagnosis, others only reached it 33 years later. However, once that threshold was reached, the steady march of progressive disability after that was very similar in everyone.

Factors That Influence Neurodegeneration

MS is a remarkably individual disease. Unlike other illnesses, it is impossible for doctors to predict the symptoms that will occur, the severity of the disease course, and if and when disability will occur. Every person is different. As mentioned above, some people may have relapsing-remitting MS for thirty years or more before they begin to progress while others experience early disabilities.

Many factors appear to influence how MS will develop during the course of one's lifetime. Disease-specific factors, such as the extent of disease activity, and the size and location of CNS lesions, also appear to be important in determining the types of disabilities that may occur and the pace at which MS will progress. . . .

Genetic susceptibility seems to play a role. There is no single MS gene—at least one hasn't been isolated—that causes MS but genetics factors do influence the immune system hyperresponse seen in MS, the amount of disease activity, how damaging the inflammatory attacks will be, and how quickly and how well that damage is repaired.

While these genetic factors are notoriously difficult to identify, further research into these factors may provide some guide posts for treatment approaches that may be beneficial in the future. . . .

Shifting the Goal Posts

The idea that there is a disease process—neurodegeneration—underlying the development of disability in MS is less than a decade old but it has already received intense interest from the research community. Neurodegeneration is a complex process and at this stage there are more questions than answers. How does nerve degeneration occur? How are axons transected and can this process be influenced? How do oligodendrocytes, the cells responsible for producing new myelin, repair damaged myelin and why are they less able to do the job as time passes? Are there ways to stimulate the body's natural repair mechanisms to restore nerve functioning? . . .

Thus far, the reduction of inflammation has been the main goal of treatment. But . . . the ability of a medication to prevent or reduce neurodegeneration is becoming the truer measure of treatment success. The new goal post for therapy is whether a medication can protect the nerves in the brain and spinal cord from deteriorating and causing disability during the course of MS.

CHAPTER 2

Issues Concerning Neurodegenerative Disorders

Neurodegenerative Diseases Are Not as Separate as Their Diagnostic Criteria Indicate

Jill Stein, Ted Schettler, Ben Rohrer, and Maria Valenti

Although various neurodegenerative disorders have traditionally been considered separate diseases, the same symptoms occur in many of them, and in most cases there are no laboratory tests that distinguish them. Furthermore, the same types of brain damage are found in individuals diagnosed with different diseases, and the amount of damage does not always correspond to the extent of a person's disability. Having multiple forms of damage is a better indicator of impairment than the type of damage. Neurologists no longer believe all such disorders are distinct from each other, yet they are still officially defined that way even though patients do not fit neatly into these categories.

Jill Stein is a physician and environmental health expert; Ted Schettler is a public health physician; Ben Rohrer is a neuroscientist; and Maria Valenti is executive director of Greater Boston Physicians for Social Responsibility.

SOURCE: Jill Stein et al., "Chapter 5: Classification Controversies in Neurodegenerative Disease," *Environmental Threats to Healthy Aging*, Greater Boston Physicians for Social Responsibility, 2008, pp. 59–61, 64–65. Copyright © 2008 by Physicians for Social Responsibility. All rights reserved. Reproduced by permission.

Photo on previous page. Neurodegenerative disorders affect memory and cause mental confusion, language problems, and personality changes. (© Alfred Pasieka/Photo Researchers, Inc.)

The changes in cognitive function that occur with aging range in severity from mild to devastating. Cognition remains virtually intact in some individuals as they grow older, while others become dependent on caregivers. Traditionally, different diagnoses such as Alzheimer's disease and Lewy body dementia have been thought to present with different symptoms and arise through different disease processes. However, while many different forms of neurodegenerative disease are recognized, the lines that separate one from another are often unclear. For instance, symptoms such as motor impairment and memory loss may occur in many different types of neurodegenerative disease. Motor impairment similar to that seen in Parkinson's disease is not enough to rule out other diagnoses, especially when both motor and cognitive impairment are present. Other symptoms, such as hallucinations or agitation, are also not disease-specific. Since, with few exceptions, no diagnostic laboratory tests exist that can clearly indicate the presence, absence, or category of a neurodegenerative disease, diagnoses are usually based on clinical evaluation of the symptoms.

Brain pathology—often considered the hallmark of diagnosis—can also show marked overlap among the syndromes of age-related cognitive and motor impairment. The brains of individuals with different neurodegenerative disorders show characteristic cellular and tissue abnormalities upon histological [tissue] examination. One of the earliest findings in autopsies of Alzheimer's patients was the presence of amyloid plaques and neurofibrillary tangles in the brain. Similarly, postmortem examinations of patients with Parkinson's disease revealed the presence of abnormal protein aggregates known as Lewy bodies. Later work revealed that these pathological markers were aggregates of different types of protein: amyloid plaques consisted primarily of amyloid-beta, neurofibrillary tangles of tau, and Lewy bodies of alpha-synuclein.

These early observations helped build the notion that neurodegenerative diseases are distinct in their causes and characteristics, each disorder with its own set of pathological features. However, further research cast doubt on this assumption of "one disease, one pathology" as it became clear that the brains of individuals with one form of neurodegeneration could also have the pathological markers of another.

Nevertheless, while the notion of a discrete, clear correspondence between disease states and certain pathological markers has largely fallen by the wayside, it is still embodied in the current definitions of neurodegenerative diseases. Attempting to diagnose a neurodegenerative disease using contemporary diagnostic standards can be likened to trying to fit shoes of one size to a randomly selected group of individuals: for the majority of them, the shoes will be either too big or too small, and for only a fraction of the group will they fit perfectly. By the same token, due to the diversity of symptoms and pathologies that exist in the real world, the number of instances where the tissue diagnosis perfectly fits the clinical disease is rather small. Instead of fitting into a simplistic conventional framework, many patients display clinical findings that overlap or otherwise do not neatly fit into current diagnostic categories.

Problems with Either-Or Definitions

When classifying neurodegenerative diseases, an initial question is "how much is enough?" When a patient first presents with abnormal neurological findings, symptoms may be mild and nonspecific and the course that the condition will take is often unclear: will the symptoms grow progressively worse, will they subside, or will they not change at all? The associated neuropathology is also unknown initially and, depending on the condition, may remain unknown or unrevealed until much later, perhaps at postmortem examination. In some neurodegenerative disorders, health and disease may be separated by shades of gray. Neurological changes build up gradually over time, and clinicians frequently ask how severe symptoms must be or how much pathology is necessary to apply a disease label.

A second problem relates to categorizing or naming the disease. When more than one possible diagnosis exists for a given set of symptoms or tissue pathologies, which one is appropriate? Neurodegenerative disorders sometimes defy rigid classification and subjective judgment is often unavoidable in the diagnosis of these conditions.

Despite the limitations of the current framework of neurodegenerative diseases, it at least offers a starting point for understanding this wide range of conditions.

The one disease–one pathology framework naturally led to the investigation of the role of pathological markers in their respective disease processes. However, research has consistently shown that pathological markers do not always correlate well with clinical findings, and that some individuals with extensive neuropathology may retain relatively intact neurological function while others with less extensive pathology may be significantly impaired. This relatively poor correlation has led some to question the value of relying too heavily on these markers for diagnostic purposes. Reflecting this uncertainty, pathologists often ask the clinician about the nature and extent of neurological impairment during life before labeling a neurodegenerative disease postmortem.

> **FAST FACT**
>
> Some scientists believe that both the circumstances of early life and environmental factors such as nutrition, physical activity, and exposure to chemicals have an impact on the brain that affect its resilience, thus influencing the timing of onset and progression of neurodegenerative disorders.

Multiple Pathologies

Although the correlation between the extent of single kinds of pathological markers and clinical symptoms is relatively poor, the presence of multiple kinds of pathology

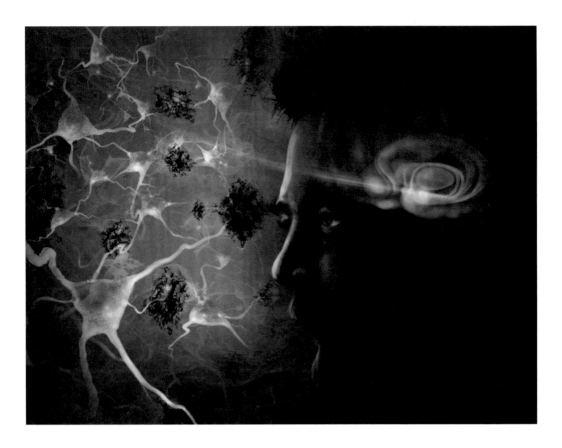

This illustration shows brain lesions called amyloid plaques that develop in areas of the brain related to memory and cognition. The plaques, which are believed to cause Alzheimer's symptoms, are protein fragments that interrupt communication between neurons. (© Jim Dowdalls/Photo Researchers, Inc.)

may be a much better predictor of the degree of cognitive impairment. A recent community-based study that compared cognitive status with pathology found that subjects whose brains had the pathological markers of more than one disease type were by far the most likely to have shown signs of cognitive impairment during clinical evaluation. While the presence of amyloid plaques was the greatest single predictor of cognitive impairment, plaques were also commonly found in cognitively healthy subjects. Of the subjects that fulfilled the neuropathological criteria for Alzheimer's disease, fewer than half actually had cognitive impairment. In contrast, mixed pathologies such as amyloid plaques with Lewy bodies or vascular infarctions [tissue damage], were rare in persons without dementia. The authors concluded that having multiple disease pathologies conferred a nearly threefold increased risk of dementia compared to having only one type of pathology. Although all studies of the correspondence between clinical symptoms and neuropathology are limited by some degree of subjectivity inherent in the current protocols for disease classification, other community-based studies have produced similar findings.

Although the notion of one disease, one pathology has long influenced thinking about dementia, neuroscientists and clinicians now increasingly address the possibility of a major role for multiple pathologies and the disease processes that drive them. The number of published studies on this topic is still relatively small, and more work is needed to elucidate the contributions of multiple brain pathologies to dementia, particularly with respect to how they may interact. . . .

Age-Associated Cognitive Impairment

Adherence to traditional disease categories and dichotomous definitions of disease (which label individuals as either "sick" or "not sick") may have contributed to current challenges in diagnosing and studying neurodegenerative conditions. For example, disease misclassification in epidemiologic studies adds to the difficulties in consistently identifying risk factors for specific conditions.

Current uncertainties have inspired some neuroscientists and clinicians to suggest that neurodegenerative diseases characterized by abnormal protein deposits should be viewed as existing along a continuum of symptoms and pathologies rather than as discrete entities. Such a spectrum of neurological impairment could better represent the heterogeneity within diagnostic categories as well as the many pathways by which different individuals can arrive at the same condition.

It is worth noting that the pathological markers themselves are not necessarily the cause of the underlying disease and clinical symptoms. Instead they may actually be a response to other antecedent disease processes, although it is entirely possible that at some later time, the pathological markers may actually begin to contribute to disease progression in a positive feedback loop. A more detailed look at the pathology associated with diseases represented along this spectrum reveals not only abnormal protein deposits but also widespread evidence of an underlying chronic inflammatory reaction characterized by activated microglia and up-regulation of various inflammatory markers. This suggests that a closer look at the origins of oxidative stress and inflammation more generally may help to identify environmental factors that increase susceptibility to neurodegenerative diseases.

Many Neurodegenerative Disorders Are Caused by Failure of Neurons to Get Rid of Waste

The Economist

Many neurodegenerative diseases have been found to result from misfolded proteins, protein molecules that are wrongly shaped and can do damage if not removed from the brain. The process of folding is complex, and mistakes sometimes occur; normally, imperfect proteins are eliminated by a structure called the proteasome. When the disposal system fails, the misshapen proteins accumulate and lead to disease. Infection of the brain with abnormal proteins called prions is one of the things that can cause this; when it does, the result is one of the rare disorders called prion diseases. Scientists are learning that other diseases, such as Alzheimer's and Parkinson's, although not prion diseases, may originate in a similar way.

The Economist is a weekly international news and business publication originating in Great Britain.

Seemingly different diseases can sometimes share a common cause. Tumours of all sorts, for example, are clusters of cells run out of control, dividing incessantly. Over the past decade, another unifying medical principle has emerged. It holds that many diseases of the central nervous system—including Alzheimer's, Huntington's and Parkinson's diseases—also share a mechanism. Instead of non-stop proliferation, the theme in this case is rubbish-disposal gone wrong.

The garbage in question is abnormally folded proteins. These are usually collected by dustmen (molecules called "ubiquitins" that pick up proteinaceous litter) before being taken to the cell's waste-processing centre (a structure known to biologists as the "proteasome"). Healthy cells create plenty of junk that keeps the system busy. The hundreds of steps of folding that create a complex protein can take a cell many minutes to complete. And with so many steps, mistakes often occur, or toxins push a perfectly configured protein out of place. Such wrongly wrought proteins need to be binned [discarded] before they cause substantial damage.

In the current [mid-September 2007] issue of the *New England Journal of Medicine*, Alfred Goldberg of Harvard Medical School, who helped discover the proteasome 20 years ago, discusses what happens to this waste-disposal system when the brain is infected by a particularly nasty protein called a prion. Prions cause Creutzfeldt-Jakob disease (or "mad cow disease" in cattle) by rearranging the structure of normal proteins in their own image. Recently scientists have started to think that prions might also disrupt the rubbish-disposal system, and that such interference might explain how they destroy nerve cells in the brain. Dr Goldberg proposes that globules of prions plug the

FAST FACT

A small number of neurodegenerative disorders are known as prion diseases because they are caused by abnormal forms of proteins called prions. All of them are rare, and most affect animal species rather than humans. Some are genetic, but Creutzfeldt-Jakob disease (the human form of mad cow disease) is infectious.

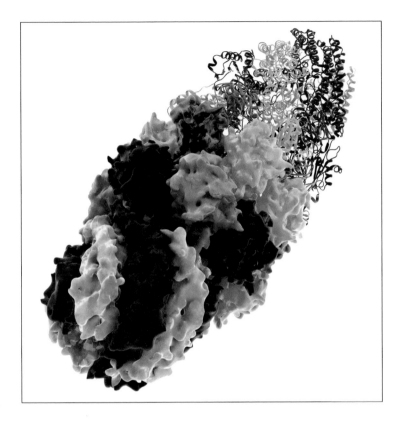

Protein waste is recycled in the cell's waste-processing center known as the proteasome, shown here. A breakdown in this process may be a cause of neurodegenerative disease. (© Ramon Andrade/Photo Researchers, Inc.)

waste-processing proteasome. That would cause all cellular garbage disposal to cease. Trash would thus remain in the brain until the accumulating filth killed the nerve cells.

Deadly Origami

Sarah Tabrizi of University College London, and her colleagues, have also examined the question of how prions kill nerve cells, transforming the brain into a spongy organ riddled with holes. They used a Petri dish of mouse nerve cells and a fluorescent lamp. The cells they studied had been modified to produce a waste protein that glows green under fluorescent light.

First Dr Tabrizi infected the nerve cells with disease-causing prions. Doing so made them grow more luminous as their waste proteins accumulated. Then she added an antibody that cleared the cells of prions but left the ubiquitins, the proteasome and the waste proteins in place. As expected, this made the nerve cells dim because they had regained the ability to dispose of their fluorescent rubbish.

A similar experiment using living mice gave corresponding results. When the mice were infected with prions, ubiquitins collected in their brains. Those ubiquitins were pinned to proteins destined for destruction but, after prions had entered the brains, the junk somehow survived.

Although these tests show that prions can force the waste disposal system to malfunction, they did not identify which part of the process went wrong. So, to work out whether the dustmen were on strike or whether the rubbish-crunching centre had been closed down, Dr Tabrizi purified some proteasomes and took a closer look. By carefully measuring the rate at which proteasomes laboured, she found a clear correlation: as the clumps of prions in the sample got bigger, the proteasomes slowed down. Thus it is the rubbish dump that ceases to work rather than the dustmen neglecting their duties.

That infectious prions cause rubbish to accumulate in brain cells may not be the only way in which they cause damage. Alex Greenwood of the Technical University of Munich, in Germany, and his colleagues, have another idea. They believe that infectious prions might wake viruses that lie dormant in the DNA of an uninfected cell.

Dr Greenwood also works with cells taken from mice. These cells contain disabled viruses because murine [mouse] ancestors, just like human ones, accumulated them in their genomes whenever infections entered their sex cells. Those historical viruses have been largely disabled by evolution over many millions of years, but they remain, they are numerous, and their genomes constitute about 10% of the DNA of most mammals.

Like Dr Tabrizi, Dr Greenwood infected several types of mouse nerve cells with prions. Next, he examined those cells to see whether they started making the previously dis-

Disposal of Misfolded Proteins

Abnormally folded protein molecules must be disposed of by a structure called the proteasome to prevent them from causing damage to the body.

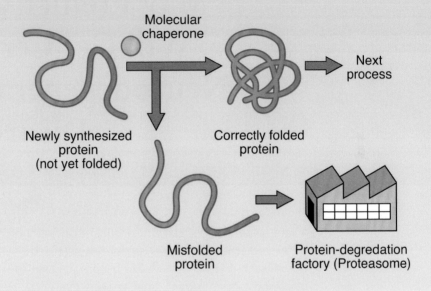

Molecular chaperone

Next process

Newly synthesized protein (not yet folded)

Correctly folded protein

Misfolded protein

Protein-degredation factory (Proteasome)

Taken from: National Institute of Advanced Industrial Science and Technology (AIST). "Discovery of a New Quality-Control Mechanism for Proteins Synthesized in Cell" (translation of the AIST press release of November 30, 2005). www.aist.go.jp/aist_e/latest_research/2006/20060104/20060104.html.

abled viruses. He found some in which this was happening. When he added an anti-prion drug to the mix, though, the virus production halted. The research is reported in *Biochemical and Biophysical Research Communications.*

Dr Greenwood's data support the theory that prions stimulate brain cells to make viruses that natural selection long put to bed. He thinks that these viruses might even transport prions between nerve cells, spreading the infection to other parts of the brain. If that idea proves correct, prions would be more than flying pickets that closed municipal dumps. They would be muck-spreaders too.

A Rare Sleep Disorder May Predict Who Will Get Certain Neurodegenerative Disorders

Megan Brooks

A rare sleep disorder called idiopathic rapid eye movement sleep behavior disorder (RBD) can be the first sign of a neurodegenerative disease that will not present other symptoms for many years, researchers have learned. Studies show that nearly everyone who has RBD will develop Parkinson's disease, Lewy body dementia, or multiple system atrophy if he or she lives long enough. This is considered an important discovery because in the future, with new treatments such as gene therapy, it may become possible to prevent the neurodegenerative disease before it appears. Meanwhile, doctors wonder whether to tell RBD patients about their potential for future development of neurodegenerative disorders.

Megan Brooks is a writer for Medscape, an online medical information source.

I diopathic rapid eye movement sleep behavior disorder (RBD) may be the initial manifestation of the synucleinopathies Parkinson's disease (PD), dementia with Lewy bodies (DLB), and multiple system atrophy (MSA), occurring some 50 years before the neurodegenerative syndrome clinically manifests, a new study suggests.

This finding has "important implications for epidemiologic studies and future interventions designed to slow or halt the neurodegenerative process," write Bradley F. Boeve, MD, and colleagues from the Department of Neurology at the Mayo Clinic College of Medicine in Rochester, Minnesota.

"Astonishing" Findings

In an interview with *Medscape Medical News*, Mark W. Mahowald, MD, coauthor of an accompanying editorial called the findings "astonishing; you can have the symptoms of RBD as a harbinger of underlying neurodegenerative disease that will take 50 years to declare itself."

"It is certainly our clinical impression now that virtually all people who have RBD that is not drug induced will likely eventually go on to develop one of the neurodegenerative disorders if they live long enough," added Dr. Mahowald, of the Sleep Disorders Center, Hennepin County Medical Center, in Minneapolis, Minnesota. "If a neuroprotective medication is identified," he added, "the data to date are so great that as soon as RBD became apparent you would place that person on that neuroprotective medication."

Using the Mayo Clinic Medical Records Linkage System, the researchers identified 550 patients with idiopathic RBD and a synucleinopathy. Twenty-seven (4.9%) of these patients met the study criterion of isolated RBD predating by more than 15 years the onset of PD, PD dementia (PDD), DLB, or MSA. Twenty-four (89%) of the 27 patients were male.

According to the Mayo Clinic team, the interval between RBD and subsequent neurodegenerative syndrome ranged up to 50 years, with a median interval of 25 years. The median age at onset of RBD was 49 years (range, 21–60 years), and the median age at onset of neurologic symptoms was 72 years (range, 51–80 years).

At initial onset, primary motor symptoms were seen in 13 patients—9 with PD, 3 with PD and mild cognitive impairment (MCI), and 1 with PDD, whereas primary cognitive symptoms occurred in 13 patients—10 with probable DLB and 3 with MCI. One patient presented with primary autonomic symptoms and was diagnosed as having MSA.

At the most recent follow-up, 63% of study subjects had progressed to dementia (PDD or DLB), and concomitant autonomic dysfunction was confirmed in 74% of all patients.

The study authors note in their report that the 27 cases of RBD predating clinically manifest neurodegeneration were collected over only 5 years, "suggesting that these long intervals of RBD preceding motor/cognitive/autonomic symptoms are not rare." They emphasize, however, that nothing can be inferred about true incidence or prevalence because this was a convenience sample from a referral database.

FAST FACT

RBD affects fewer than one out of two hundred persons, generally beginning in late middle age.

RBD and Neurodegeneration

"Initially, RBD was just felt to be kind of a curious clinical observation," Dr. Mahowald told *Medscape Medical News*. "Then it became apparent that the majority of people who develop RBD will eventually go on to develop one of the synucleinopathies, particularly Parkinson's or dementia with Lewy bodies."

Dr. Mahowald and colleagues were the first to document the relationship of RBD and these neurodegenerative disorders. They reported that nearly 40% of

Typical Clinical Features of REM Sleep Behavior Disorder

- Male gender predilection
- Mean onset age 50–65 years (range 20–80 years)
- Vocalizations, swearing, screaming
- Motor activity varies from simple limb jerks to complex motor behavior, with injuries to patient or bed partner
- Dreams often involve attacks by animals or humans
- Exhibited behaviors mirror dream content
- Behaviors tend to occur in latter half of the sleep period
- When associated with neurodegenerative disease, RBD often precedes dementia and/or Parkinsonism by years or decades

*Note: REM = rapid eye movement; RBD = sleep behavior disorder.

Taken from: Bradley F. Boeve, Michael H. Silber, and Tanis J. Ferman. "REM Sleep Behavior Disorder in Parkinson's Disease and Dementia with Lewy Bodies." *J Geriatr Psychiatry Neurol* 2004 17:146. Reprinted with permission from Boeve B, Silber M, Ferman T, et al., "REM Sleep Behavior Disorder in Parkinson's Disease, Dementia with Lewy Bodies, and Multiple System Atrophy." In: Bedard M, Agid Y, Chouinard S et al., eds. *Mental and Behavioral Dysfunction in Movement Disorders.* Totowa, NJ: Humana Press, 2003. http://jgp.sagepub.com/content/17/3/146.full.pdf.

patients with isolated, idiopathic RBD later went on to develop a parkinsonian disorder after a mean of about 13 years.

"What's really astonishing about this [new] study from the Mayo Clinic, which I think is very credible, is that the interval has been extended to 50 years," Dr. Mahowald said.

The Mayo Clinic study, he and colleagues note in their editorial, confirms "one of the most interesting mysteries—the overwhelming male predominance (89% in this study) of those with RBD who develop a neurodegenerative process, which is not male-predominant." The reasons for this are unknown. Hormonal studies have not implicated androgenic [male] hormones.

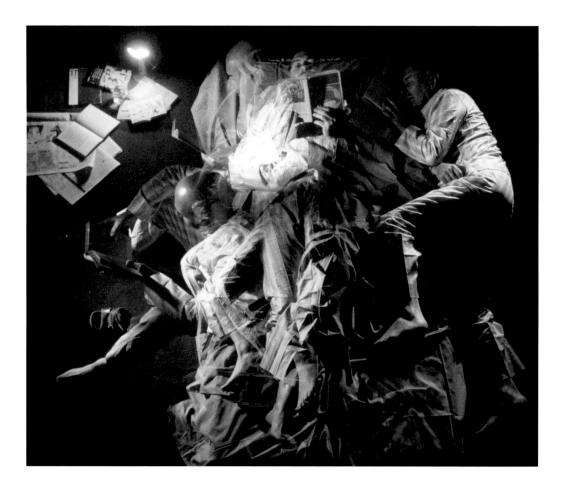

A rare sleep disorder called idiopathic rapid eye movement sleep behavior disorder may signal potential neurodegenerative disease in later years. (© Oscar Burriel/Photo Researchers, inc.)

The finding that RBD may be a very early warning sign of neurodegenerative disease has important implications for treatment, Dr. Mahowald said, given "exciting new treatments" for PD that are on the horizon, such as gene therapy and cell replacement therapy.

"But the sad fact is that by the time Parkinson's disease becomes clinically apparent there has been widespread damage in the central nervous system that has probably been going on for decades," Dr. Mahowald said. "We have to come up with an extremely early marker for Parkinson's disease if these new therapies are going to work, otherwise the horse is out of the barn. "Idiopathic RBD may absolutely be such a marker," he predicted.

To Tell or Not to Tell

In an interview with *Medscape Medical News*, Dr. Boeve acknowledged that there is some debate among neurologists about what to tell patients with RBD. "When you make a diagnosis of RBD," he noted, "should you talk with them about the potential development [of neurodegenerative disease] down the road?"

Dr. Boeve thinks you should, in most cases. "Patients are not dumb," he said. "They are going to Google RBD and it just makes sense to say, 'this is what has been observed by a number of investigators, we don't have prediction abilities at the moment, but a lot of research programs around the world are intensely looking at this.' A lot of them want to participate in this research," he noted.

Using Adult Stem Cells in Research on Neurodegenerative Diseases Avoids Controversy

Stephen Falconi

If stem cells could be transplanted into areas of the brain where neurons have died, this procedure might lead to effective treatments for neurodegenerative disorders; however, stem cell research has been extremely controversial because it has been done mainly with cells obtained from embryos, the use of which is objectionable to people who oppose abortion. Now scientists are learning to harvest stem cells from the bodies of adults. Neural stem cells, which would be needed for transplantation into the brain, are more difficult to harvest than those from other parts of the body because so far there is no technique for extracting them without risking damage to surrounding brain tissue. If such a technique can be developed it will mean great progress toward development of cures.

Steven Falconi is a science writer whose work has appeared in the online magazine *Nvate*.

When stem cell research emerges in conversation, it inevitably creates controversy. Some view it as if stem cells were conjured up by [gothic authors] Emily Brontë or Bram Stoker for some frightening science-fiction tale. Others in the scientific and medical communities describe its potential to cure a who's who of chronic and terminal conditions. The controversy casts a pallor over the whole field of stem cell research, but not all stem cells are created equal—a new sub-field, adult stem cells, could provide the benefits of embryonic stem cells but sidestep the ethical debate.

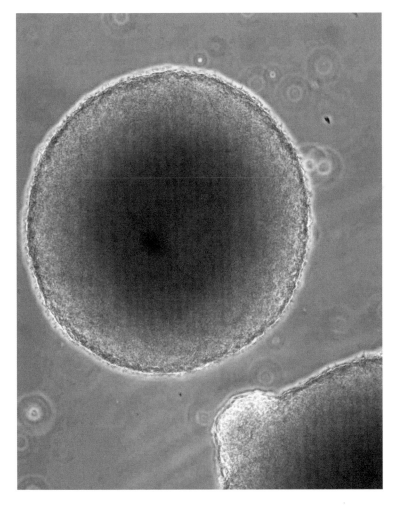

A light micrograph of a human neural stem cell. Neural stem cells may be able to replace damaged or lost brain cells in those with neurodegenerative disorders. (© Riccardo Cassiani-Ingoni/Photo Researchers, Inc.)

Nearly half a million Americans suffer from Parkinson's disease, a horrific neurological condition characterized by tremors, delayed motion, loss of automatic movement, muscle rigidity, and dementia. While there are many pharmaceutical treatments for Parkinson symptoms, there is no cure for the degeneration. Parkinson's only worsens with time, and those suffering from the disease have little hope for improvement. Huntington's disease, also a brain-degenerative disorder, is characterized by jerky, involuntary movements, disabled balance and coordination, depression, blunted emotion, and dementia. Like Parkinson's, Huntington's has no cure, and its victims usually die within 10 to 30 years of diagnosis. Huntington's disease in particular affects a very specific part of the brain—the striatum, which is involved in movement coordination. If stem cells could be transplanted into affected areas, they could replace brain cells that are degenerating or dead.

We're often told that stem cells come from aborted fetuses, and if you oppose abortion, you must also oppose stem cell research and treatment. It is true that stem cells *can* be harvested from aborted embryos. However a new, promising source of stem cells is the adult human being. Scientists can now harvest tissue-specific stem cells from numerous locations in the adult body—bone marrow, mammary glands, and even parts of the brain—specifically the subventricular zone and hippocampus. The pluripotency (cell's ability to differentiate into specific tissues) is surprisingly high for these adult stem cells.

Adult Neural Stem Cells

Marrow stem cells can be used to treat blood and marrow diseases, in addition to certain cancers. Most intriguing for scientists are the possibilities for neural stem cells. If

> **FAST FACT**
>
> Stem cells are unspecialized cells that have not yet developed into a specialized cell type. Because they are unspecialized, they are able to become one of many types of specialized cells, such as heart muscle cells, blood cells, or nerve cells. This process is called differentiation.

we could effectively harvest, maintain, and transplant these stem cells, we could replace neurons in the brain destroyed by degenerative conditions like Parkinson's and Huntington's disease, as well as traumatic brain and spinal cord injuries. Neural stem cells are practical because they can be easily maintained in a laboratory, and they multiply in a very short amount of time, giving scientists a large pool of donor cells from which to choose.

How Adult Stem Cells Are Harvested

Adult stem cells can be taken from blood drawn from one of a person's arms while the other components of the blood are reinfused into the other arm. However, this does not work for neural stem cells. Before they can be widely used to treat neurodegenerative diseases, a safe way must be found to obtain them from the brain.

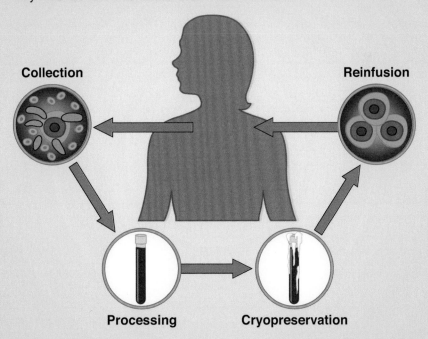

Collection

Reinfusion

Processing

Cryopreservation

Taken from: Denis Rodgerson, Ron Rothenberg, and Wayne A. Marasco. "New Hope for Curing Degenerative Diseases." *Life Extension Magazine*, October 2007. www.lef.org/magazine/mag2007/oct2007_report_stem_cells_01.htm.

Adult stem cells still face hurdles. One obstacle is that harvesting these cells is incredibly difficult because their locations in the body require risky and invasive techniques for removal. Scientists must find techniques to extract neural stem cells without damaging brain structures surrounding them—a difficult task to say the least. This barrier, like so many in modern medicine, will come down with enough research. Small steps are being made to treat neural degenerative disorders. While the research is tedious, the possibilities are truly incredible. Adult stem cells could be the final riddle to finding viable treatments for an impressive host of neurological disorders.

The Issue of Driving with Parkinson's Disease Is Controversial

Kate Kelsall

The issue of whether it is safe to drive is a controversial and emotional one among people with Parkinson's disease (PD). Driving requires a great many skills that are affected by the disabilities PD causes, such as reduced reaction time, visual-spatial orientation problems, and muscle stiffness. Medication for PD can cause sudden sleep onset. So PD patients must drive carefully and take precautions to compensate for their physical problems. Among those Kate Kelsall has adopted are switching from a stick shift to an automatic, driving only in the daytime, avoiding freeways, turning the radio off, and driving without passengers. Independence is important to her, so she wants to retain her ability to drive as long as possible.

Kelsall maintains a blog with information about PD. She has worked both as a certified public accountant and as a social worker.

SOURCE: Kate Kelsall, "The Controversy Surrounding Driving with Parkinson's," *Shake, Rattle and Roll: An Insider's View of Parkinson's Disease and DBS,* August 31, 2008. http://katekelsall .typepad.com. Copyright © 2008 by Kate Kelsall. All rights reserved. Reproduced by permission.

Y ou might think that the most controversial Parkinson's disease-related topic involves politics like the stem cell controversy, sexual obsessions and compulsions from dopamine agonists, or a religious quandary (Why me, God?). [But] the most controversial issue is driving with Parkinson's disease. Writing about this emotionally charged topic feels like writing about end-stage Parkinson's disease—gut-wrenching and anxiety provoking.

Joseph Friedman, M.D. thinks the topic of driving with Parkinson's disease (PD) is so important that he devoted an entire chapter to it in his latest book *Making the Connection between Brain and Behavior: Coping with Parkinson's Disease.* Patients with PD may be unable to evaluate their own driving, while their neurologists may be overestimating their patients' abilities to drive.

Driving involves a number of activities including perception, information processing, judgment, decision-making, coordinated limb movements, reaction time tasks, continuous tracking, and attention. PD causes a number of abnormalities in these areas.

Driving with Parkinson's

Research on drivers with PD revealed a number of problems we all need to consider as we work to keep our abilities sharp. *Reduced physical and mental reaction time* is due to bradykinesia (slowness of movement). PD patients are slow performing most tasks, and may react to emergency situations with more delay than people without PD. It may be difficult to react quickly to a road hazard.

Visual-spatial orientation problems can result in:

• Problems judging distances (e.g., gauging the distance to a stop sign or traffic light)
• Keeping the car in the correct lane
• Driving too far to one side of the road
• Difficulty scanning the road

• Difficulty spotting and interpreting traffic signs
• Problems identifying roadside landmarks
• Difficulty distinguishing shapes

Concentration difficulties are common among people with Parkinson's disease, and they also have difficulty

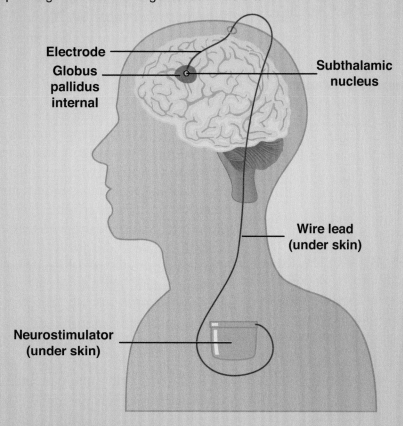

Deep Brain Stimulation for Parkinson's

Deep brain stimulation (DBS) is a way to block impulses from the brain that cause Parkinson's disease tremors. Electrodes placed in the brain are connected to a neurostimulator that is implanted under the skin of the chest. This device sends electrical pulses up through wires to the target areas in the brain.

Electrode

Globus
pallidus
internal

Subthalamic
nucleus

Wire lead
(under skin)

Neurostimulator
(under skin)

Taken from: The Dana Foundation. "Parkinson's Disease—The Dana Guide."

attending to multiple tasks. Naturally distractions from passengers, radio, and traffic can be taxing.

Fatigue and sudden sleep attacks while driving are often caused by PD medications, particularly dopamine-agonists. Patients who are excessively sleepy fall asleep suddenly, and have no recollection of being drowsy before falling asleep.

On-off fluctuations in physical symptoms due to PD medications.

Muscle stiffness contributes to:

- A limited range of motion, particularly in the neck
- Dystonia (muscle-cramping) in the toes
- Rigid muscles that affect the ability to turn the steering wheel, use the gas pedal, push down the brake, and make quick movements

Strengthening Driving Skills

With PD, my driving skills are a little more limited, and I need to compensate. Driving is important to me to maintain my independence and self-esteem. I fear the isolation and dependency when I stop driving. To keep me and others safe on the road I've come up with some compensation strategies.

A couple of years ago, I traded my stick shift car for an automatic which has helped with my multi-tasking problems. Some of my PD driving problems have lessened with deep brain stimulation (DBS) surgery and with proper programming of the neurostimulator. I no longer have muscle-cramped toes while driving (you can imagine how difficult it was to push down the gas pedal or hit the brake pedal). Also, my on-off fluctuations in medications have decreased. Fortunately, the sudden sleep attacks I experienced as a passenger in a car (and thankfully not as a driver) have stopped, because I've discontinued taking Mirapex, a dopamine agonist.

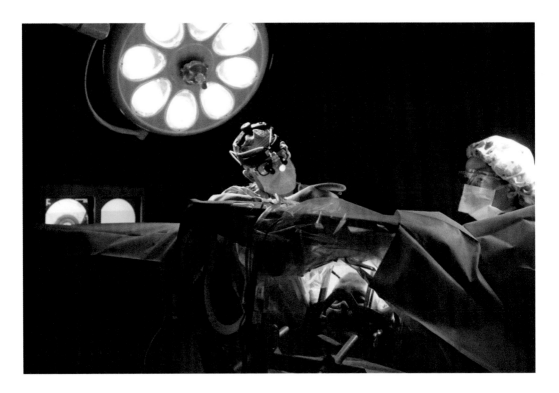

I've also set limitations and choose to restrict my driving by:

- Planning my itinerary before leaving the house
- Driving in the day only
- Driving on well-known routes and back roads, and avoiding the freeways, if possible
- Driving when there is less traffic
- Driving in good weather conditions, if possible—no snow, ice, or heavy rain
- Driving without passengers
- Avoiding distractions by turning the radio and CD player off (It's obvious, but I should mention no eating or using a cell phone while driving.)

Researching the topic of driving with PD has scared me into enrolling in the AARP [American Association of Retired Persons] course, 55 Alive Driver Safety Program. To improve my driving skills, I will also contact

A brain surgeon performs deep brain stimulation on a conscious patient. (© Michael Ventura/ Alamy)

the Association of Driver Rehabilitation Specialists. Once the snow stops pounding in Colorado, I intend to take an on-road driving test through a private driving organization.

I want to confront this taboo topic of driving with Parkinson's disease. By understanding and dealing with my deficits as a driver with Parkinson's disease, I can update my driving skills, or recognize when the time comes to give up driving altogether.

All People at Risk for Huntington's Disease Have the Right to Reproductive Procedures

LaVonne Goodman

People with close relatives who have Huntington's disease may have inherited the gene for it, and genetic tests can reveal whether this is the case. But some people at risk choose not to be tested because they feel it would be too upsetting to know they will eventually develop the disease when there is no way to prevent it. They may nevertheless want to be sure that their children will not get the disease. Through medical reproductive procedures, they can choose to have only children who will not, but there is some risk attached to these procedures. A debate has arisen about whether the procedures should be used without first testing to determine whether they are needed. Some authorities have taken the position that such testing should be required, but others believe that only the couples involved have a right to decide.

LaVonne Goodman is a physician and patient advocate with special interest in Huntington's disease. She and her husband are the founders of Huntington's Disease Drug Works, which focuses on research and available treatments.

SOURCE: Dr. LaVonne Goodman, "The Right Not to Know: PGD for Huntington's," *Huntington's Disease Drug Works*, January 1, 2010. http://hddrugworks.org. Copyright © 2010 by Huntington's Disease Drug Works. All rights reserved. Reproduced by permission.

*W*ho has the right to decide how couples at risk for Huntington's should have children? Or more specific to the debate now occurring in Europe: What rights do couples have when requesting reproductive procedures (PGD) for the purpose of having a gene negative [without the Huntington gene] child? What are the issues in this debate—and who has the right to decide?

What is PGD [preimplantation genetic diagnosis]? Medications are given to the woman that will stimulate the development of multiple eggs. When mature, the eggs are retrieved with a needle and are then incubated with the male partner's sperm. On day 3 of embryo development, a small number of cells are tested for the Huntington gene (this is the PGD part) then a few days later the non-HD embryos are placed in the woman's uterus by a very common, low-risk procedure (IVF [in vitro fertilization]) frequently performed in fertility clinics.

PGD has been offered to Huntington couples—and to couples at risk for other genetic diseases—so that they can decrease the risk of passing a disease gene to their child. Up to this point PGD for Huntington's has been an option for couples with one partner who is known to be gene positive, *and* for couples with one partner at risk [that is, one who has a relative with Huntington's disease] who chooses not to know—or to learn—personal gene status prior to or during PGD procedures.

What Is the Debate?

The controversy concerns only those at risk couples who choose not to know their own gene status (PGD with non-disclosure). PGD in this situation can result in 3 different possibilities:

If the at risk parent is gene positive and a gene negative embryo has been identified, it can be selected for the IVF procedure. The gene status of the parent is not disclosed and remains unknown to the parent.

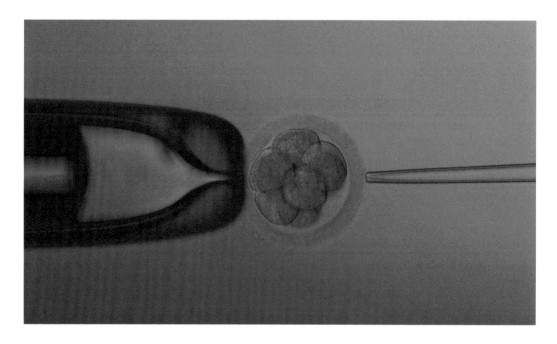

If the at risk parent is gene positive and a gene negative embryo can't be identified (when only gene positive embryos are available) it becomes more problematic. Though this is not a common situation, doctors may: (1) repeat the procedure for obtaining embryos, in which case the gene status of the parent is more likely to become known, or (2) perform a "sham" IVF procedure that delivers no embryo. In this situation gene status is not disclosed, but the woman partner undergoes an unnecessary procedure—one which has potential to harm.

If the at risk parent is gene negative, there would be no need for PGD, and as in the former case, the woman partner undergoes an unnecessary IVF procedure which has potential to harm.

There are those who argue—as did members of the committee of the International Huntington's Association (IHA), and groups of medical and legal professionals in the UK and the Netherlands—that it is not ethical for doctors to perform sham or unnecessary PGD-IVF procedures for couples whose choice is not to know gene

A colored light micrograph shows a human embryo during preimplantation genetic testing for the Huntington's gene. (© Pascal Goetgheluck/ Photo Researchers, Inc.)

status. In fact the government in the Netherlands now *requires* gene testing in order to qualify for embryo selection by PGD for Huntington's.

What Is the Counterargument?

On the other side, there are those who argue that couples at risk for HD have the right not to know genetic status, and that it is not ethical to restrict their options for PGD. The authors in a recent article in *The Journal of Medical Ethics* review exactly this question. The major points:

They cite the "Universal Declaration on the Human Genome and Human Rights", a legal document agreed to by the United Nations which states that it is: *"The right of every individual to decide whether or not to be informed of the results of genetic examinations and the resulting consequences should be respected."*

They also discuss the potential risk of harm and the psychological burden that may be caused by genetic testing in HD in the particular situation where the couple would choose not to know. They cite the increased short-term (within one year) psychological risk of catastrophic life events, including suicide, when compared to those who test negative or the general population. In those who are forced to test, the risks may be greater. Though it has not been studied, the authors suggest "that undesired knowledge may influence life plans substantially; it may induce depression or close off life plans that would otherwise have been considered, or frustrate fruitful life plans already in place".

Therefore they argue that there may be substantial risk for harm in forcing couples to test for HD prior to PGD.

Other Issues

There are two separate but related issues in this PGD debate. The first deals with balancing the risks for harm in

> **FAST FACT**
>
> Although everyone with the gene for Huntington's disease will eventually develop symptoms (failing earlier death from some other cause), scientists believe that environmental factors may play a significant role in the age of onset and the speed at which symptoms progress.

How Generic Neurodegenerative Diseases Are Inherited

Many neurodegenerative disorders are at least partially the result of genetic predisposition. But some, such as Huntington's disease, are entirely genetic, so that it can be determined even before birth whether a child has inherited a gene that will cause the disease to appear sooner or later. The defective gene can come from either parent.

Autosomal Dominant Inheritance

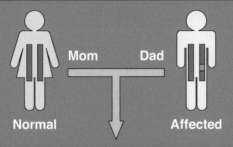

Mom   Dad

Normal   Affected

Each child inherits a normal copy of the gene from Mom, and either a normal or defective copy from Dad

Possible combinations:

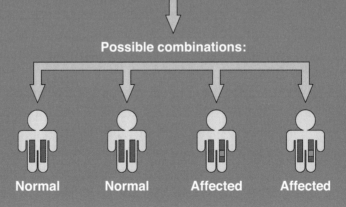

Normal   Normal   Affected   Affected

	Autosomal (nonsex) chromosome with normal copy of gene
	Autosomal chromosome with defective copy of gene

Taken from: Genetic Sciences Learning Center, University of Utah. "What Is Huntington's Disease?"
http://learn.genetics.utah.edu/content/disorders/whataregd/hunt.

this situation: the risks related to unnecessary medical procedures against the risks of forcing gene testing. This sort of balancing of risk and benefit is what happens (or should) in every medical encounter calling for informed consent—whether it is a newly prescribed medicine or a surgical procedure. The second deals with whose right it is to decide: Does it belong to the couple, the government, or a Huntington's organization?

Huntington families know—better than anyone else—that there are no easy life decisions for those at risk. Do we dare encourage serious relationships, or work toward careers that may be disrupted by HD? What about marriage? And probably the most difficult, what about children? Like every thing else in HD, PGD is a hard decision that does not have a clear right or wrong answer. But I will argue along with the United Nations that the right of decision—to test or not—belongs to the couples involved.

It is also legitimate for individual doctors who object to PGD for gene untested couples to refuse to perform the procedure. But in this setting PGD centers have responsibility to identify other doctors who are willing. This type of compromise is nothing new; it already occurs with other difficult medical situations like abortion and death with dignity initiatives; doctors have the right to participate or not.

And finally, it is my opinion that the International Huntington's Association needs to reconsider their proposed (I believe paternalistic) guideline that recommends against PGD for Huntington couples that choose not to gene test. And I would go further and say they may have it backwards: they should be advocating *for* the rights of Huntington's families—not proposing they be taken away. And yet further on my wish list: They could be a positive international force advocating *for* insurance coverage for the many Huntington couples who would choose this procedure as an option for having children—but can't afford it.

A Controversial New Treatment for Multiple Sclerosis Is Being Sought by Patients

Steven Novella

A new theory about multiple sclerosis (MS), proposed by Italian surgeon Paolo Zamboni, is attracting attention from MS patients, many of whom are traveling to foreign countries to receive treatment based on it. Zamboni believes that MS is caused by chronic cerebrospinal venous insufficiency (CCSVI); that is, insufficient blood drainage from the brain resulting from blocked veins. This theory has not been scientifically proven, although researchers are investigating it, and it will be many years before it can be validated. Nevertheless, some patients maintain that the clearing of blocked veins has improved their condition or even cured it. A number of them claim that neurologists and pharmaceutical companies have conspired to suppress the CCSVI theory. So far, the evidence obtained from studies does not support the CCSVI theory, but more research is needed.

Steven Novella is a clinical neurologist at Yale University School of Medicine. He is the president of the New England Skeptical Society and the host and producer of the weekly science podcast *The Skeptics' Guide to the Universe.*

There is an interesting controversy raging in the Multiple Sclerosis (MS) world that reflects many of the issues we discuss at [the website] Science-Based Medicine. Dr. Paolo Zamboni, an Italian vascular surgeon, has now published a series of studies claiming that patients with clinically defined MS have various patterns of chronic cerebrospinal venous insufficiency (CCSVI). Further Dr. Zamboni believes CCSVI is a major cause of MS, not just a clinical side-consequence, and is exploring treatment with venous angioplasty [clearing of blocked veins] or stenting [a tube inserted into a blood vessel to keep it open].

The claims have captured the attention of MS patients, many of whom have a progressive course that is only partially treated by currently available medications. There are centers popping up, many abroad (such as India), providing the "liberation procedure" and anecdotes of miraculous cures are spreading over the Internet. There is even a Facebook page dedicated to CCSVI, and you can read the anecdotes for yourself. Many profess dramatic improvement immediately following the procedure, which seems unlikely even if Zamboni's hypothesis is correct.

Zamboni is also getting attention from neurologists and MS specialists, who remain skeptical because Zamboni's claims run contrary to years of research and thousands of studies pointing to the current model of MS as an autoimmune disease.

There are at least two stories to follow here. The first is the scientific story—the questions being proposed are answerable with scientific research, and they will be answered. MS remains a serious illness that is inadequately treated (not to downplay the important advances we have made, but we certainly are far from an adequate cure for MS). The potential of a new treatment deserves serious research attention, and CCSVI is getting it. It will probably take another ten years for the research to play itself

A Controversial Treatment for Multiple Sclerosis

Some doctors believe that multiple sclerosis is caused by a condition called chronic cerebrospinal venous insufficiency (CCSVI), although this theory is generally considered unproven. It consists of insufficient drainage of blood from the brain because of blocked veins. A number of patients have reported that the symptoms have improved after they have undergone treatment to open their veins. This treatment, called angioplasty, is more commonly used to open veins to the heart.

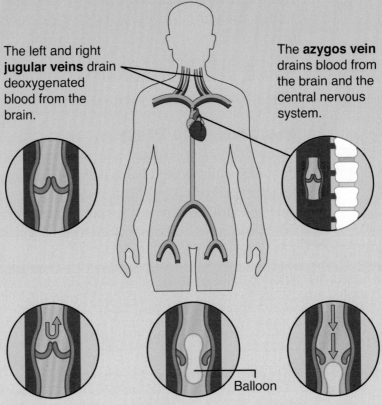

The left and right **jugular veins** drain deoxygenated blood from the brain.

The **azygos vein** drains blood from the brain and the central nervous system.

Balloon

Before
In blocked jugular or azygos veins, the valve obstructs blood flow from the brain and spine to the heart.

During
A catheter is inserted into the vein and threaded to the valve. A balloon is inflated and loosens the valve.

After
The catheter and balloon are removed. Blood flows through the vein without obstruction.

Taken from: "Hope—and Concern—in New MS Treatment." *Orange County Register*, October 10, 2011. www.ocregister.com/articles/patients-320934-procedure-veins.html?graphics.

out adequately for there to be a confident consensus on CCSVI, but eventually we will have a scientific answer.

The other story is the the reaction of the public and the MS community. This has been mixed, but already there are conspiracy theories that the neurology community, the MS society, and Big Pharma [the pharmaceutical industry] (of course) are fighting against CCSVI as part of a misguided turf war. Anecdotes are being used to argue against published scientific evidence, and negative studies are being dismissed. If CCSVI is eventually found to be a scientific dead end, I have to wonder if it will survive as just another fringe "alternative" treatment, like Laetrile, psychomotor patterning, and other discarded ideas in medicine.

The Scientific Story

So far there is not much of a scientific story to tell. A PubMed [online medical database] search on CCSVI yields a total of 19 publications (a pittance), indicating how new this concept is. I suspect this number will grow into the hundreds at least before this story plays itself out.

This stent is inserted into a blocked vein or artery to keep the blood vessel open and blood flowing through it. (© Clouds Hill Imaging Ltd./Photo Researchers, Inc.)

If CCSVI is proven to be legitimate then this number will grow into the thousands over the next few decades. If it is disproved, publications will trickle off.

Most of the current research is published by Zamboni's team. He is building an impressive list of studies, exploring various aspects of CCSVI and MS, but evidence that derives entirely from a single research team is always suspect. The role of bias in research is well documented, and, further, most new ideas in medicine turn out ultimately to be wrong. Therefore skepticism is the proper approach to bold new claims being supported by a lone research team. Replication will be necessary for the broader scientific community to take CCSVI seriously.

The core claim made by Zamboni is that most patients with MS display 2 or more out of 5 criteria on studies of venous anatomy (using ultrasound or venography) of venous insufficiency [completely or partially blocked veins] while control patients (healthy subjects or those with other neurological disorders) display 1 or no criteria, and never 2 or more. All other claims (benefit from angioplasty, matching patterns of venous insufficiency with types of MS) derive from this core claim.

I found four independent replications in the literature, three very recently published. . . .

One of four replications found results similar to Zamboni. A second found only 20% of MS patients met Zamboni's criteria, while two others found that no patients with MS did. Four studies is not a lot—and is not even close to ending this controversy from a scientific point of view. But these early results are not promising and will tend to deepen skepticism within the neurological community.

FAST FACT

The National Multiple Sclerosis Society estimates that there are about four hundred thousand people with MS in the United States. Its prevalence varies by geographic location even within the United States, and still more widely around the world, so it is believed that environmental factors and ethnicity play a role in causing the disorder.

More Research Needed

Clearly there is a need for more research so that both patients and professionals can feel comfortable that CCSVI has been given a thorough investigation and we can say with confidence what role, if any, it plays in MS. The results, also, do not have to be black and white. While it seems unlikely that Zamboni has discovered the sole and ultimate cause of MS in most or all patients, it is possible he has found a significant consequence of MS. Chronic inflammation may result in venous insufficiency in some patients. This venous insufficiency may further play a role in worsening the clinical course in a subset of those patients, who may benefit from treatment. So CCSVI may ultimately play a minor but important role in the management of MS.

Or it may all turn out to be a figment of Zamboni's imagination, spawned by the sincere hope of finding a cure for MS. Time and research will tell.

My open plea to the MS community, especially those who are going down the rabbit hole of conspiracy theories, is to keep this discussion about the scientific evidence. This is not the place for cheap conspiracy theories. I fear my plea will fall on deaf ears, but it never hurts to ask.

A High School Student Looks Back on Caring for His Great-Grandmother

Max Wallack

Max Wallack's great-grandmother had Alzheimer's disease. From the time he was six or seven years old, he felt responsible for her and took part in caring for her. Although he loved her very much, the fact that she could not be left alone limited the things his family could do. Eventually she became so confused that she thought her caregivers were trying to kill her and tried to escape from the house at night. At the age of ten, Max slept by her side and helped to pick her up when she fell out of bed. For many years he read about her condition and tried to understand it; now he plans to become a geriatric psychiatrist so he can help other Alzheimer's patients and their caregivers.

Max is a student at Boston University Academy. He is the founder of Puzzles to Remember, a project that provides puzzles to nursing homes and veterans institutions that care for Alzheimer's and dementia patients.

Photo on previous page. Caring for a person with a neurodegenerative disorder is a full-time job. (© Marmaduke St. John/Alamy)

I consider myself to be a responsible person. I credit my caregiving of my great grandmother for my sense of responsibility. The earliest I can remember definitely feeling responsible for Great Grams was when I was 6 or 7.

Great Grams lived with us, and I felt great love for her. We were friends. Having no brothers or sisters, she was almost a sibling in her relationship with me. As I saw her begin to fail, I spent long hours trying to explain things to her. I think she was less threatened by receiving help from me than from an adult. We were friends.

On the other hand, many things we did were limited by Great Gram's inclusion. Often, it was not so much that we didn't want to include her, as that she herself was fearful of many people and events and didn't want to participate. Unfortunately, we couldn't leave her alone, which often meant foregoing events.

When I was 7 or 8, I was constantly aware of her inability to do the kinds of things that many of us take for granted. Whenever we went anywhere, I stayed with Great Grams. If that wasn't possible, I often insisted that some other family member stay right with her. Clearly, I assumed a caregiver role. It was never assigned to me by my family. I just did what was needed and necessary.

I thought things were difficult in that early stage, but I had no idea what the future would bring. One of the most difficult things for me was witnessing the horrible burden all of this was placing on my grandmother. More and more, the whole family stayed all together in order to support each other.

Difficult Nights

I spent many nights sleeping on the floor, even though my home and room were just around the corner.

This became very difficult when Great Grams ceased to sleep at night. The problem was clear, but the solution was elusive. Everyone was tired. Great Grams would fall asleep many times during the day. We knew we should try to keep her awake during the day, but everyone was so tired that it was a relief when she fell asleep, so we would use the time to do other things we needed to do. Then, of course, night came and it was time to pay the price.

Great Grams would often try to escape at night. She would even put her nightgown over her underclothes and slip, so she would be "ready" for her flight. Great Grams didn't wander. She wasn't looking for something. She was trying to escape. Perhaps, she was trying to escape her own terrible mental situation.

Great Grams would often call the police, or run to security officers, and tell them that we were trying to kill her. I have often wondered if other Alzheimer's caregivers have encountered this. I know many Alzheimer's patients can act mean to their caregivers, but I have never heard of any other patient who constantly felt the caregivers were trying to kill her.

Physically, Great Grams was a small, but strong person. She still had the ability, 6 months before her death, to run down a hill to a main street, flag down a truck, and get the truck driver to take her to the police station. However, her physical abilities began to fluctuate, just as her mental abilities fluctuated.

Finally, she began to fall when she got up a night. By the time I was ten, I was helping pick her up from the floor at night. She would even climb out of a hospital bed with sides. That was my life, at that point—a ten year old boy helping pick up from the floor a half naked 95 year old woman, on a regular basis.

In Great Grams' more lucid moments, I was her greatest source of joy. In her more lucid moments, she was concerned about my well-being. In her confused moments, she was my sibling rival, competing for attention and jealous of any attention that I received.

A Sense of Commitment

I spent many years trying to help Great Grams. I spent many years reading about and researching her condition. I wanted to understand more. The more I understood, the more I could overlook her difficult moments, appreciate the moments when she was "more there", look beyond the disease, and recognize the great grandmother who no doubt had great love for me.

My emotions during those years were clearly conflicted. Someone whom I loved was making my life very difficult. Someone I loved clearly needed my help, but didn't always appreciate it.

People on the Alzheimer's Reading Room [website] have sometimes addressed the question as to whether sometimes they wish it were "all over". I can only remember thinking that one time. That was a time when my grandmother was so worn down and ill that I wished she would be freed of the care of Great Grams. I didn't want to lose Great Grams, but, at that moment, I would have chosen to relieve my grandmother.

There is no question—this is a very difficult disease. It brings with it many responsibilities and ethical dilemmas. I don't think anyone can go through being a caregiver to an Alzheimer's patient and not come out a stronger and more responsible person. I didn't realize it then, but my personality and sense of commitment were being formed during those difficult years.

Now I am committed to spending my life helping care for Alzheimer's patients and their caregivers. I will be the kind of geriatric psychiatrist that takes into account the entire family, because I know that the entire family is affected. Most of all, I will really care because I have been there.

A Woman Describes the Mental Tasks That Help Her Cope with Multiple Sclerosis

Janine Lodato

Janine Lodato is physically disabled by multiple sclerosis, but her mind is sharp and she engages in many activities that require using her brain. She writes, watches DVD movies, listens to books on tape, and plays word games with her husband. She uses many assistive technologies to interact via the Web, such as a voice robot and a laser-activated keyboard that she can control by moving her head. She feels that she is a very lucky person because she has the support of her husband and of family and friends.

Lodato has had multiple sclerosis for more than twenty-five years and has published articles about ways people can cope with it.

To compensate for a total loss of motor skills due to Multiple Sclerosis (MS), I have focused on the development and performance of mental tasks. I write articles. I create books, I play Scrabble with my caregiver husband, I watch DVD movies and documen-

SOURCE: Janine Lodato, "Mind Gym," E-bility.com, January 13, 2010. http://www.e-bility.com. Copyright © 2010 by Dweloda, Inc. All rights reserved. Reproduced by permission.

taries from Netflix, a great service indeed, and listen to magazines and books on tape provided by the Library of Congress, another worthwhile service to people with disability, delivered at no charge.

I am absolutely sure I am avoiding the onset of cognitive problems, dementia and Alzheimer's. I firmly believe that using my brain in activities requiring the mind will continue to keep me productive in spite of my severe physical disability. My husband even jokes that I am causing him to lose his memory because I remember all the phone numbers, all the names, all the activities in which we have participated, so he gives himself permission to forget such information.

There are things I can still do such as think, talk, observe, feel, react, compose: all mental functions. I have been forced to concentrate on the mind oriented activities.

People around me marvel at how I seem so normal, even though I am very physically limited I am also very mentally active. Yes, I have a disability, but my mind and emotions still work fine, maybe even better.

Assistive Technology

My husband reminds me frequently that "no one is disabled when on the Internet, when one interacts via the Web". So I use him as my VoxBot (voice robot) and Key-Bot (a keyboard robot) when I want something quick via the Web. Also I use voice recognition software and soon will be using a laser-activated keyboard brought to me from New Zealand made by a company there called LO-MAK [Light Operated Mouse And Keyboard].

This innovative keyboard functions with a laser attached to a cap on my head. Most people with a disability can move their heads. The LOMAK laser-based keyboard is linked to a simple tablet computer, a PDA, made by NouvoNet, located in Silicon Valley.

Since I cannot turn my body myself in bed, I consistently wake my husband up so he could roll me from one side to the other or scratch my nose and perform many other little but important functions. I do this three or four times each night.

He tells me he does not mind that his sleep is disrupted so frequently, because this allows him to remember four times as many dreams versus just one which would be the case if he slept through the night [with] no interruptions. Normally we only remember the very last dream of the night when we wake up.

He likes to induce his dreams by means of concentrating on an important subject he wants to think about or solve. He does this focused concentration as he is about to go to sleep. He is convinced that he becomes four times more productive due to my repeated interruptions of his sleep.

He also told me that he would like a LOMAK keyboard on our ceiling above our bed so he could keyboard a few keywords, specific to the subject he wants to dream about. He would do this just as he is about to fall asleep. Then the computer would, with a Sleep Induction software, recognize that he just wants to search for the keywords. The computer would automatically connect to Google then would text to voice the 3 top results even while he is sleeping, increasing the potential of the specific dream he would like.

He is crazy, of course, or is he?

I am the luckiest person on the face of the earth, as Lou Gehrig [a famous baseball player who had amyotrophic lateral slerosis, or ALS,] so appropriately announced in his farewell speech, that I am surrounded by the support of my hero husband, my family and my friends and they all appreciate my mind and ignore my physical disability.

An Astronaut's Journey with Parkinson's Disease

Rich Clifford

Rich Clifford, an astronaut for the National Aeronautics and Space Administration (NASA), learned to his surprise that he had Parkinson's (or Parkinson) disease when he went for a routine flight physical. He had no noticeable disability, and at his request he was not only assigned to a space shuttle mission but was allowed to perform the space walk for which he had been preparing. Realizing that the press would create unfavorable publicity for NASA if his condition were known, he did not divulge it publicly until long after he left to become the Boeing space station flight operations manager and then deputy program manager of Boeing's space shuttle program. Since the end of the shuttle program he has been speaking for the National Parkinson Foundation to encourage others with Parkinson's and has won the 2012 Public Leadership in Neurology Award from the American Academy of Neurology.

SOURCE: Rich Clifford, "An Astronaut's Journey with Parkinson's Disease," National Parkinson Foundation, 2012. http://www.parkinson.org. Copyright © 2012 by Michael Richard Clifford. All rights reserved. Reproduced by permission.

It was just past midnight on March 14, 1996. I began the day strapped into the crew compartment of a space shuttle headed for orbit. I was minutes away from the launch of shuttle mission STS-76, and I could hear the voice of launch control counting off the seconds until finally I heard, "3, 2, 1 and liftoff of the shuttle *Atlantis* on a mission to the Russian MIR space station." That pre-dawn launch was my third space shuttle mission as a United States Astronaut. It was, however, my first mission to space after being diagnosed with early Parkinson disease (PD).

It seems improbable if not impossible: an astronaut with PD had not only been certified for space flight, but had also been certified to perform a planned space walk on the MIR space station. That morning, as I began the ascent into orbit to rendezvous with the MIR, I thought about my own personal journey leading up to that moment. It was as hard as any I'd ever faced, but one that I had never given up on. A journey that had begun almost two years earlier.

My second mission had been STS-59 in April 1994 and it was very successful. I felt completely fit during and after the flight. About six months later I went in for my annual flight physical. Everything, including my standard neurological exam, was satisfactory. Just as a favor, I asked the flight surgeon after the exam if I could have an orthopedic surgeon look at my right shoulder. (I played competitive racquetball and thought I might have recently injured it during a game). He asked me where it hurt and I told him it didn't hurt at all. Rather, my right arm just seemed to hang without moving when I walked. I could tell I must have touched a nerve (no pun intended) because he immediately called for the Chief Flight Surgeon. The Chief asked me to walk with him down the hall. Little did I know how that walk would change my life. The next thing I knew, the Chief informed me that he was taking me into Houston the next day to see an expert at the Medical Center. I was surprised at the sudden and ominous turn of events, as I had assumed my visit would have yielded a quick fix and allowed me to resume my competitive racquetball. That's when the Chief informed me I was going to see a neurologist, a man by the name of Doctor Joseph Jankovic. I assumed this was part of the normal sequence to get my arm fixed.

A Shocking Discovery

I was surprised by the urgency of the visit, and more than a little confused when, after taking a careful history and examining me, Dr. Jankovic informed me that I had PD. I had never heard of this disease and as someone who considered himself to be in excellent physical condition, I naturally assumed it was something I could conquer. In fact, my response was something like, "OK, fix it so I can get back to my racquetball!" Then, reality hit me. Hard! The doctors explained I had several tests ahead of me. PD was a clinical diagnosis and confirmed only by eliminating—through tests—all other neurological disorders. Needless to say, racquetball was no longer on my list of priorities.

The test results came back negative. The doctors were right: I had PD. But my only symptom was that my right arm didn't move when I walked. It seemed impossible. I didn't want to believe it, and for a while I refused to believe it.

So many things went through my head when I began to learn more about my condition, but I was resolute and determined not to let it affect my outlook. The medical community respected my privacy and only those senior NASA managers with a need to know were informed. They asked me what I wanted to do, and my response was quick: I wanted to remain on flight status and remain in the [queue] for a future space flight. I wanted to remain an astronaut.

According to researchers, PD is a progressive degenerative disease that occurs over time. That meant it was very likely that I had PD prior to my first shuttle flight STS-53 in December 1992. I saw no limitations to what I could do just because I had PD, and I used all of the available research to build a case for why I should continue to fly. Thankfully the NASA flight surgeons, senior NASA management, and my family supported me, and I was granted return-to-flight status under the condition that I would be watched closely by the flight surgeons. I also knew that I could not disclose my condition publicly.

Back to Space

Keeping this secret between myself and those closest to me, I was subsequently assigned to STS-76. I was to be a member of the crew, but was told I would not be assigned to perform the planned space walk (extra-vehicular activity, or EVA, in NASA speak). I, along with another astronaut named to the STS-76 crew, had performed the majority of the development testing of hardware and operational procedures for the experiment packages to be deployed during the planned space walk. In other words, knowing as much as we did about the subject, our expectations were that we would be assigned to perform the EVA. I informed management that I wanted to do the EVA and that I didn't know there were limitations imposed on my capabilities. I think they were actually surprised by my desire to perform the space walk, despite my condition.

Before long, they reassigned me the EVA. The mission was highly successful, including the six-hour long EVA during which my crewmate and I attached four MIR Environmental Effects Payload experiments to the station's docking module to better understand the environment around MIR over an 18-month period.

Looking back, I recognize the difficult decision NASA senior management made in assigning me to STS-76. I am thankful to have had the full support of the Flight Surgeons, Dr. Joe Jankovic, and Johnson Space Cen-

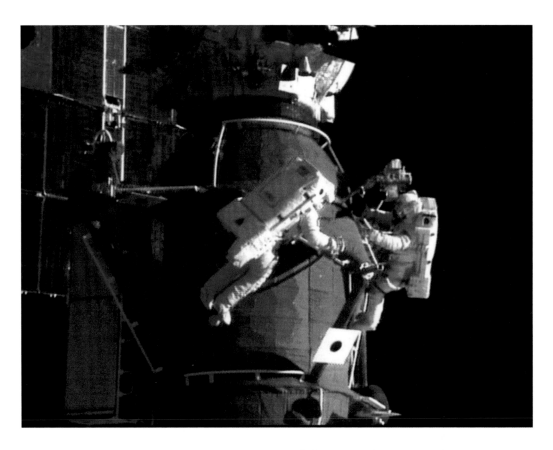

Astronaut Rich Clifford, left, works on the Mir space station during a 1996 space walk. Clifford went on the space mission despite having been diagnosed with Parkinson's.
(© AP Images/NASA TV)

ter management. They presented my capabilities to the NASA Headquarters Space Flight Medical Review board and I know it was not an easy decision for the board and senior management to clear me for flight. I am grateful for their support in realizing the risk they took with me when there were dozens of other qualified astronauts who could have performed this mission. It is a testimony to their certification processes that they were assured I could perform the mission.

An Active Life

And although no one ever restricted me from going public with my PD, I knew it was best to remain quiet at the time. Too many questions of the managers and medical review board by an inquiring press would have proven to be embarrassing for all of us. I could imagine the focus of the typical question, "How could you let someone with Parkinson disease fly in space?" I am forever appreciative for the opportunity these people afforded me. They took the high road instead of making the easy decision, which would have been to ground me permanently.

With this article I have now gone public. Following my third and final space shuttle mission, I left NASA in January 1997 and joined the Boeing Company as Space Station Flight Operations Manager. In 2007 I became the Deputy Program Manager of Boeing's Space Shuttle Program, a position to which I am committed until the Space Shuttle fleet's retirement in 2011. In writing this article, I hope to inspire others with PD by showing them that Parkinson is not the end of your life. I believe that mental limitations are defined by what you make of your situation. In the famous words of former NASA Flight Director Gene Kranz, "Failure is not an option." I am continually reminded of this by my best support group: my wife Nancy and my sons Richard and Brandon. Without their encouragement I probably would have followed a different path.

It has been 17 years since I received my initial diagnosis. I left the Astronaut ranks in 1997 for reasons not associated with PD. The disease has progressed as you would expect but its acceleration is following a very low ramp, thanks to the help of my doctors and continued advances in PD research. I am still active in the workforce and play golf as often as I can. All in all, I am far from giving in to the limitations of PD, but rather I'm planning to—as the late Paul Harvey said at the start of each of his radio shows—"stand by for the rest of the story."

A Long-Term ALS Patient Believes His Life Is Worth Living

Joe O'Connor

In the following selection Joe O'Connor writes about Steve Wells. Wells is Canada's longest-living survivor of amyotrophic lateral sclerosis (ALS). He is fifty-one and was diagnosed thirty years ago, when he was twenty-one, whereas only 10 percent of ALS patients survive more than ten years. He lives in a hospital since he is paralyzed and cannot move his limbs or speak. But he can write, using a computer that enables him to compose messages by selecting one letter at a time with his eyes. He works as a self-employed stock market trader. And life is meaningful to him. He does not consider himself sick, and believes that anything is possible if you have the courage to follow your dreams.

Joe O'Connor is a reporter for the Canadian newspaper the *National Post*.

SOURCE: Joe O'Connor, "'There Are Too Many Things That Can Be Done'; Thirty Years After His Diagnosis, Canada's Longest-Living ALS Patient Is Doing More than Simply Surviving," *National Post*, April 23, 2011. Copyright © 2011 by the National Post. Material reprinted with the express permission of: Joe O'Connor and National Post, a division of Postmedia Network Inc.

His arms are discoloured, and skinny as a child's. They lie, palms down, on a table. His legs are likewise emaciated, robbed of any discernible muscle mass. There is a blue terry cloth bib around his neck, clipped in place to catch the saliva that occasionally bubbles from between his lips. His breathing is shallow. He is silent as a stone. No movement. No words.

Looking at him, sitting there, trapped in a tomb of a body and surrounded by the dull white hum of the hospital ward in Toronto's east end [in Ontario, Canada,] where he lives, I think how awful his life must be, how difficult, how incredibly sad. My pity misses the point. My pity has no idea who it is dealing with.

"The one thing that I truly despise is people feeling sorry for me," Steve Wells writes in one of the many responses he delivers to my many questions. "I don't feel sorry for me. Why should anyone else?"

The Progression of ALS

His hands were the first body part to go. That was when he was in his 20s. Then his right foot began to "slap," before his entire right side fell apart. Gradually his speech slurred. It was a slow process. But it never stopped. It doesn't. That's the thing with amyotrophic lateral sclerosis [ALS], more commonly known as Lou Gehrig's disease, a neuromuscular nightmare that attacks the nerve cells in the brain and spinal cord and shuts down its victims' bodies, piece by piece—and for which there is no cure. Eighty per cent of ALS victims are dead within two to five years of diagnosis. Ten percent survive beyond 10 years, while five percent live to see 20 years, post-diagnosis.

And then there is Steve Wells. He was 21 when the doctors delivered the bad news. He is now 51, turning 52 in October [2011], and Canada's longest-living ALS survivor. He is a statistical anomaly, cheating death in a game of life where the disease always wins, and he cannot help but feel an unenviable distinction.

Accepting Reality

"Is my longevity fate?" he muses, typing out his thoughts on a computer screen, one sentence at a time, using a program he operates with his eyes. "No. It just is what it is: a very stubborn and determined guy who refuses to give in. Part of accepting the illness is, at least for me, an acceptance of reality. As such, I really don't spend much time wishing that I could do something that can't be done. Because there are, quite simply, too many things that can be done."

Mr. Wells is a self-employed day trader, a stock market gambler. Lately he has been betting (and winning) with gold. He navigates the markets and communicates to the world beyond—and the visitor at his elbow—by using "Eyemax" technology. His computer system, in effect, locks onto his gaze. On one screen is an image of a keyboard. His eyes flick from letter to letter. Words appear in a white space to be read, saved and sent as email correspondence. For brevity in face-to-face encounters Mr. Wells has a simple system: one blink means yes. Anything else means no. A smile is a smile. And he smiles often.

Trading stocks from a hospital room using space age, eye-operated gadgetry was not the future he envisioned growing up in Thunder Bay [Ontario]. He imagined he might be a statistician, or a draftsman, or maybe a psychologist—a university major he joked about in his parting comment of his high school yearbook, saying it would teach him all he needed to know about getting dates. He was a jock, after all, and it was in his second year of a Phys Ed degree at Queen's University when doctors explained why he could no longer throw a perfect spiral with the football anymore.

He had a disease. And there was no cure. After diagnosis, instead of devastation, he got right back into it: Chasing romance. Doing assignments. Playing flag football. He credits his parents, John and Joan, for his attitude. They taught Steve and his younger sister, Laurie, to accept the things they cannot change—and get on with it. Which is what he did. He completed his degree, moved to Toronto, found an apartment and took a variety of jobs, from selling cars to working at an athletic apparel and shoe store. "I don't know how many customers I scared away while attempting to tie the laces of their shoes," Mr. Wells writes.

By 1993, when he was 34, he had "retired" from his job as a travelling salesman for an international fruit company. Within a year, he could no longer walk. By 1998, he could no longer speak. He was 39.

Daily Care and Simple Pleasures

After years of relative independence, Mr. Wells had to enter the world of total care. In 2003, he moved to his current address at Toronto East General Hospital. "It was a very difficult transition, difficult not only for me but for the nurses as well," he admits. "I had always taken responsibility for my care."

At 1:15 p.m., a nurse appears. Lunchtime. She adds water to a protein and caloric powder, stirs it and pours the solution into an intravenous bag hanging from a hook above the patient's wheelchair. His intravenous diet is fine-tuned to his individual tastes. It includes the kind of staples every stockbroker requires: caffeine in the morning and an ice-cold beer or a dollop of Scotch after work.

Simple pleasures. There are others: Friends, family (his father passed away a few years ago, his sister and mother remain close and live in the area), the smell of fresh air, travel (Europe, Scandinavia, Central America and numerous Caribbean hotspots), a lively joke and Alsie. Alsie Jones is a nurse. (Not at the hospital). The couple met several years ago and enjoy an intimate relationship, both in mind and body. Mr. Wells describes her as the "silver lining" in his ALS.

A Deeper Meaning

He sees his life in flashes. Brilliant bursts where everything is clear. At the time he was diagnosed, for example, Terry Fox [an athlete and amputee] was running his marathon of hope. Mr. Wells, then just 21, feeling fine, but recently diagnosed with an incurable disease, spotted the one-legged runner on the highway near Wawa, in Northern Ontario. He slowed the car.

"The next two seconds haunt me to this day," he writes. "I felt his pain. His drive. His determination. And I understood all of it, immediately." He said he instantly felt that his own life had a special purpose, a deeper meaning. He was not sure what it was. He still isn't sure he knows now. It might have nothing to do with ALS. Or it could be that the disease is his calling. Living with it, longer than anyone else in Canada, longer than the imagination allows, and not allowing it to define him. "I don't consider myself sick, although my sense of humour is sometimes referred to as such," Mr. Wells types, in our long correspondence. "Rather, I'm just navigating around different potholes in the road of life."

He is not religious, does not pray to any God. He has faith, though, in himself, and in a glass–half full perspective. "I have always been an optimist," he writes. "The disease is only physical, so anything is still possible if you have the courage to follow your dreams. It takes a while to learn that."

Making the Most of Life

I ask about assisted suicide. ALS sufferers are among its leading advocates. Sue Rodriguez famously fought for the right to die, taking her case to the Supreme Court of Canada, where she lost 5–4 in 1993. A year later an anonymous physician helped end her life.

Mr. Wells saw her death as a "cop out." "I am for assisted suicide when someone has no hope of regaining consciousness or is brain dead," he writes. "Other times I would have to consider it on a case by case basis. . . . Suicide, or a do-not-resuscitate order, has never been part of my thinking process."

The phone rings. It clicks over to the answering machine. It is a brokerage house with a message for "Mr. Steven Wells." He has a couple of trades that need to be completed by the closing bell. It is time to get back to work. I stop by the nurses' station on the way out. Mention the patient in room 511 and the staff members smile. The doctors can't explain him. They don't even try.

It sounds like something from a self-help manual, but you meet Steve Wells and share a few laughs (his on the inside) and walk away feeling uplifted. Affirmed by what is possible, not saddened by what he has lost.

"ALS doesn't have to be seen as an automatic death sentence," he writes. "Lou Gehrig said: 'I may have been given a bad break in life, but I consider myself the luckiest man alive.' That embodies my core belief. Life is what you make of it."

Pity misses the point.

A Husband Describes the Problems of Living with a Wife Who Has Huntington's Disease

Kevin Jess

Kevin Jess's wife has Huntington's disease. This not only causes physical problems, such as walking in such a way that she appears to be drunk when she is not; the worst part is that the neurodegenerative damage to her brain has affected her mind. She becomes very agitated and sometimes violent and often believes that something is in the house that would harm her, such as large snakes or a fire. Though she could be helped by medication, she denies that she is sick and refuses to take it. Jess has to work from home in order to give her the constant attention her condition requires. Their nine-year-old son cannot remember a time when his mother was normal, but Jess recalls sadly what an active and accomplished woman she used to be.

Kevin Jess blogs at DigitalJournal.com and lives in Kingsport, Nova Scotia, Canada.

Life with someone who has Huntington's disease [HD] is difficult to say the least, but what if the victim of this disease is in denial? How does this affect the person afflicted and how does it affect the family and friends who are closest to them? Realistically, I can only speak from personal experience as my wife is one of those who is in denial of this rare disease that afflicts approximately 30,000 people in the U.S. alone, according to statistics on eMed.tv. This works out to be about 1 in 10,000 with another 150,000 at a 50 percent risk of having the gene that later develops into Huntington's disease. . . .

As the disease progresses past some movement and a gait that resembles someone who may have drunk too much alcohol, leading onlookers to believe that they are drunk, the most alarming symptom is that of choking. HD affects the ability to swallow, and eating becomes a horror rather than what is a pleasure for most of us. Presently there is no cure, nor are there any treatments for the disease. There are drugs available to ease the movements that afflict patients with HD. . . . Research is ongoing and there are promising treatments now in clinical trials.

A Nightmare Experience

In our family's experience it has been a nightmare. Denial is the rule of the day. [The disease] is not talked about or referred to in any way. Since it is very easy for a person with HD to become agitated and unreasonable it is a source for conflict that is often violent in nature, so police had to be informed as well as professional caregivers.

Most nights are spent calming my wife down as dementia has been a constant occurrence. At times I spend nights pretending to toss incredibly large snakes out the door or put out fires and cure the odd sick child. I have learned that to argue would only mean more agitation on her part thus prolonging her agony.

Our family doctor is overworked but is sympathetic to our plight and has tried to make some headway only to have her shatter everything he tries by refusing tests or medications to calm down her mood swings. He calls it a "Shakespearean tragedy". Here is a woman who if she would face what she obviously has and accept treatment for the symptoms could have a much better life, but seems destined to misery for herself simply out of stubbornness and maybe even an inability to reason.

According to our family doctor, in Canada it's not easy to declare someone incompetent. The person must be able to answer three questions. What's your name? What is the date? And, where are you? She can answer all three questions. She still maintains a driver's license but I have managed to convince her that the car has problems that could make her stranded so she doesn't chance it. She chokes most meals and drinks down, walks like a drunk and says inappropriate things during conversations with friends and family. All of these are hallmarks of the dreaded monster disease. To describe the disease in terms that most can understand, I tell them this—imagine having someone in your house that has Alzheimer's, Parkinson's, and Tourette's syndrome all at the same time. In some South American countries victims of this disease are kept in makeshift jails in their homes as there are no services to help families deal with the unpredictable nature of the symptoms.

Unavoidable Changes

Due to her inability to come to terms with the disease, many things in our household have had to change. I have to work from home, pay exclusive attention to her as paranoia makes her think that she is not a priority. My 9 year old son doesn't remember when she was "normal". He doesn't remember that she ran her own restaurant, was a beautiful painter, designed her own clothing and could cook like she should own a 5 star restaurant. She was also, and still is, one of the prettiest women that I ever laid eyes on.

GLOSSARY

Alzheimer's disease (AD) The most common neurodegenerative disorder, found in many people over age sixty-five and nearly half of those over eighty-five, which is characterized by dementia.

amyloid plaques Abnormal structures made of a protein called beta-amyloid that are found in the brains of people with Alzheimer's disease.

amyotrophic lateral sclerosis (ALS) The scientific name of the neurodegenerative disease commonly known in the United States as Lou Gehrig's disease.

axon A fiber extending from the body of a nerve cell by which messages are transmitted to other nerve cells.

autosomal dominant A pattern of inheritance in which an affected individual receives one mutant gene and one normal gene on a pair of chromosomes other than sex chromosomes.

Bradykinesia Slowness of movement.

central nervous system (CNS) The brain and spinal cord.

chorea Involuntary jerking or twisting movements of a patient's feet, lower arms, and face.

cognitive dysfunction Difficulty with thinking, memory, or concentration.

Creutzfeldt-Jakob disease (CJD) A rare neurodegenerative disease caused by prions, similar in humans to mad cow disease in cattle.

DBS Deep brain stimulation, a treatment for Parkinson's disease and some other neurodegenerative disorders that involves involuntary movement.

dementia A disorder characterized by cognitive dysfunction.

demyelination	Disintegration of the nerves' protective covering.
dysphagia	Impaired chewing and swallowing.
dyspnea	Shortness of breath.
familial	In reference to a disease, this term refers to a hereditary form of the disease.
fasciculations	Involuntary twitchings of muscles.
FDA	The US Food and Drug Administration, which must approve all medications.
frontotemporal degeneration (FTD)	A neurodegenerative disease that produces dementia.
Huntington's disease	A hereditary neurodegenerative disease, formerly called Huntington's chorea.
idiopathic	Of unknown cause.
IVF	In vitro fertilization (fertilization of an egg in a laboratory dish or test tube).
Lewy bodies	Abnormal aggregates of protein that develop inside nerve cells in Parkinson's disease and DLB (dementia with Lewy bodies).
Lewy body dementia or dementia with Lewy bodies (DLB)	A neurodegenerative disease characterized by the presence of Lewy bodies.
Lou Gehrig's disease	A name used for amyotrophic lateral sclerosis, or ALS, only in the United States and Canada; named after the professional baseball player who suffered from the disease.
Mendelian inheritance	Inheritance of characteristics transmitted by specific genes in accord with Mendel's Law.
motor	In reference to diseases or symptoms, this term refers to movement or muscle weakness.

motor neuron diseases	A group of disorders in which motor nerve cells (neurons) in the spinal cord and brain stem deteriorate and die.
motor neurone disease (MND)	The name used for ALS in Great Britain and Europe.
multiple sclerosis (MS)	A demyelinating neurodegenerative disease causing total or partial paralysis and muscle tremor.
mutation	A change in the DNA nucleotide sequence of a gene.
myelin	A material that forms a protective sheath around a nerve fiber.
nervous system	The network of specialized cells called neurons that coordinate the processes of the body and transmit signals between its different parts.
neural	Relating to a nerve or the nervous system.
neurodegeneration	The breaking down of tissue in the nervous system, resulting in the dysfunction or death of neurons.
neurofibrillary tangles	Twisted fibers found inside brain cells in Alzheimer's disease.
neurologist	A physician who specializes in diagnosis and treatment of diseases of the nervous system.
neuron	A nerve cell.
neurotransmitter	A chemical that transmits signals from a neuron to another neuron, muscle, or other tissue.
nucleotide codes	Building blocks of genes arranged in a specific code that chemically forms into proteins.
parkinsonism	A neurodegenerative disorder with symptoms resembling those of Parkinson's disease that does not meet all the criteria for that disease.
Parkinson's disease (PD)	A neurodegenerative disorder marked by tremor of resting muscles, impaired balance, and a shuffling gait.

PGD — Preimplantation genetic diagnosis, a reproductive procedure.

prion — A microscopic infectious particle, composed of misfolded protein, which causes several rare neurodegenerative disorders.

progressive disease — An incurable disease in which symptoms keep on getting worse and worse.

protein — A biochemical compound that facilitates a biological function, typically folded into a globular or fibrous form.

RBD — Rapid eye movement sleep behavior disorder.

receptor — A molecule on the surface of a neuron that receives signals by means of a specific neurotransmitter.

sporadic — In reference to a disease, refers to a form of the disease that is not hereditary and appears sporadically without a known cause.

stem cell — A relatively undifferentiated cell that can divide into daughter cells that can differentiate into particular cell types (e.g., neurons).

syndrome — A collection of signs, symptoms, and medical problems that tend to occur together but are not related to a specific, identifiable cause.

TBI — Traumatic brain injury (for example, a sports injury).

vascular dementia — Dementia caused by impaired blood circulation to the brain.

CHRONOLOGY

1817 James Parkinson, an English scientist, describes the disease now known by his name.

1850 Augustus Waller, a British neurophysiologist, describes the appearance of degenerating nerve fibers.

1863 Nikolaus Friedreich, a German neurologist, first describes a progressive hereditary neurodegenerative disorder (Friedreich's ataxia).

1868 Jean-Martin Charcot, a French neurologist, describes multiple sclerosis (MS).

1872 George Huntington, an American physician, describes Huntington's disease.

1874 Charcot describes amyotrophic lateral sclerosis (ALS).

1876 Charcot names Parkinson's disease.

1892 Arnold Pick, a Czech neurologist, describes Pick's disease, a form of frontotemporal degeneration (FTD).

1906 Alois Alzheimer, a German psychiatrist, describes the amyloid plaques found in the brains of people with the neurodegenerative disease that later comes to bear his name.

1910   Emil Kraepelin, a German psychiatrist, names Alzheimer's disease.

1912   Friedrich (Fritz) Lewy, a German American neurologist, describes the abnormal protein deposits in the brain now known as Lewy bodies.

1921   Otto Loewi, an Austrian pharmacologist, discovers the first neurotransmitter.

1939   The American public becomes aware of amyotrophic lateral sclerosis, or ALS, when baseball legend Lou Gehrig's career—and, two years later, his life—is ended by the disease.

1946   The National Multiple Sclerosis Society is founded.

1957   The National Parkinson Foundation is incorporated.

1958   Arvid Carlsson, a Swedish scientist, finds dopamine to be a transmitter in the brain and proposes that it has a role in Parkinson's disease.

1963   Stephen Hawking, a British physicist, is diagnosed with ALS. He nevertheless becomes a world-renowned scientist and, as of 2012, has lived longer with the disease than any other person.

1966   The first academic Department of Neurobiology is established at Harvard University.

1967   Famous poet and songwriter Woody Guthrie dies of Huntington's disease, and his wife creates the organization that later becomes the Huntington's Disease Society of America.

1968   The first study reporting improvements in patients with Parkinson's disease resulting from treatment with L-Dopa is published.

1979   The Alzheimer's Association is founded.

1980s   Electronic augmentative and alternative communication (AAC) devices become available to patients with neuro-degenerative diseases who are unable to write or speak normally.

1981   Magnetic resonance imaging (MRI) is first used to record abnormalities in the brain and along the spinal cord.

1985   The ALS Association is founded.

1993   The gene responsible for Huntington's disease is identified.

1995   An international consortium of researchers establishes guidelines for diagnosis of dementia with Lewy bodies (DLB) and decides on that as the official name for it.

1996   Aricept, the first drug for Alzheimer's disease, is approved.

1997   Stanley B. Prusiner, an American neurologist, is awarded the Nobel Prize in Physiology or Medicine for the discovery of prions.

Early 2000s   Researchers begin to view multiple sclerosis as a neuro-degenerative disease rather than a strictly inflammatory disease as was once thought.

2004   Former US president Ronald Reagan dies of Alzheimer's disease.

2010   A genetic link is found between the familial and sporadic forms of ALS.

2011   Congress passes the National Alzheimer's Project Act (NAPA) to create a national strategic plan to address and overcome the rapidly escalating crisis of Alzheimer's disease.

2012   The World Health Organization (WHO) issues a major report on the growing worldwide problem of dementia caused by neurodegenerative disorders.

ORGANIZATIONS TO CONTACT

The editors have compiled the following list of organizations concerned with the issues debated in this book. The descriptions are derived from materials provided by the organizations. All have publications or information available for interested readers. The list was compiled on the date of publication of the present volume; the information provided here may change. Be aware that many organizations take several weeks or longer to respond to inquiries, so allow as much time as possible.

ALS Association
1275 K St. NW, Ste. 1050, Washington, DC 20005
(202) 407-8580
fax: (202) 289-6801
e-mail: advocacy@alsa-national.org
website: www.alsa.org

The ALS Association is the preeminent nonprofit organization for amyotrophic lateral sclerosis (ALS) and leads the way in global research, providing assistance for people with ALS through a nationwide network of chapters, coordinating multidisciplinary care through certified clinical care centers, and fostering government partnerships. Its website contains extensive information about the disease, plus stories of patients and several downloadable manuals on aspects of living with ALS.

Alzheimer's Association
225 N. Michigan Ave., Fl. 17, Chicago, IL 60601
(800) 272-3900
website: www.alz.org

The Alzheimer's Association works on a global, national, and local level to enhance care and support for all those affected by Alzheimer's and related dementias. It is the largest private nonprofit funder of Alzheimer's research. Its website contains extensive information on all aspects of dementia for patients, caregivers, and the public, including publications that can be downloaded. It also offers a section for teens that includes videos.

Alzheimer's Foundation of America (AFA)
322 Eighth Ave., 7th Fl., New York, NY 10001
toll-free: (866) 232-8484
fax: (646) 638-1546
e-mail: info@alzfdn .org
website: www.alzfdn .org

The AFA unites more than sixteen hundred member organizations from coast to coast that are dedicated to meeting the educational, social, emotional, and practical needs of individuals with Alzheimer's disease and related illnesses and their caregivers and families. Its branch for teens, www.afateens.org, seeks to mobilize teenagers nationwide to raise awareness of Alzheimer's disease, as well as to educate and support teens whose family members are affected by it.

Association for Frontotemporal Degeneration (AFTD)
290 King of Prussia Rd., Radnor Station Bldg. #2, Ste. 320, Radnor, PA 19087
(267) 514-7221
e-mail: info@theaftd .org
website: www.theaftd .org

The AFTD is a nonprofit organization whose mission is to promote and fund research into frontotemporal degeneration (FTD); provide information, education, and support to persons diagnosed with an FTD disorder and their families and caregivers; and bring about greater public awareness of the nature and prevalence of FTD. Its website contains information about the disorder and current research related to it.

Huntington's Disease Society of America (HDSA)
8303 Arlington Blvd., Ste. 210, Fairfax, VA 22031
(703) 204-4634
fax: (703) 573-3047
website: www.hdsa.org

The HDSA is a national nonprofit health organization dedicated to improving the lives of people with Huntington's disease and their families. Its goals are to promote and support research and medical efforts to eradicate Huntington's disease, to assist people and families affected by Huntington's disease to cope with the problems presented by the disease, and to educate the public and health professionals about Huntington's disease. It is composed of regional chapters, each of which has its own section of the national website.

Les Turner ALS Foundation
5550 W. Touhy Ave., Ste. 302, Skokie, IL 60077
toll-free: (888) 257-1107
fax: (847) 679-9109
e-mail: info@lesturner als.org
website: www.lesturner als.org

The Les Turner ALS Foundation, one of the nation's largest independent ALS organizations, is a local, national, and international leader in research, patient care, and education about ALS, serving more than 90 percent of the ALS population in the Chicago area. It conducts an annual ALS Walk4Life and other events to raise funds and public awareness. Its website contains information about its services and the current issue of its e-mail newsletter.

Lewy Body Dementia Association (LBDA)
912 Killian Hill Rd. SW, Lilburn, GA 30047
toll-free: (800) 539-9767
fax: (480) 422-5434
e-mail: lbda@lbda.org
website: www.lbda.org

The LBDA is a nonprofit organization dedicated to raising awareness of the Lewy body dementias (LBD); supporting patients, their families, and caregivers; and promoting scientific advances. Its website contains information about LBD, including reports, an archived newsletter, and other materials that can be downloaded, as well as resources for caregivers and a discussion forum.

Multiple Sclerosis Association of America (MSAA)
706 Haddonfield Rd., Cherry Hill, NJ 08002
toll-free: (800) 532-7667
e-mail: webmaster@ms association.org
website: www.ms association.org

The MSAA is a national nonprofit organization dedicated to enriching the quality of life for everyone affected by multiple sclerosis (MS). It provides ongoing support and direct services to individuals with MS and the people close to them and serves to promote greater understanding of their needs and challenges. Its website contains information on all aspects of MS, including many videos, and also offers booklets that can be downloaded or ordered by mail.

National Institute of Neurological Disorders and Stroke (NINDS)
NIH Neurological Institute, PO Box 5801, Bethesda, MD 20824
toll-free: (800) 352-9424
website: www.ninds .nih.gov

The NINDS is part of the National Institutes of Health, an agency of the US Department of Health and Human Services. It conducts, fosters, coordinates, and guides research on the causes, prevention, diagnosis, and treatment of neurological disorders and stroke and collects and disseminates research information. Its website contains detailed information about all neurological disorders, including neurodegenerative disorders.

National Parkinson Foundation (NPF)
1501 NW Ninth Ave./ Bob Hope Road, Miami, FL 33136-1494
toll-free: (800) 327-4545
fax: (305) 243-6073
e-mail: contact@ parkinson.org
website: www.parkin son.org

The NPF is a nonprofit organization focused on meeting needs in the care and treatment of people with Parkinson's disease. Its mission is to improve the quality of care through research, education, and outreach. Its website contains detailed information about the disease and the problems encountered by people who have it, plus many personal stories.

Parkinson's Disease Foundation (PDF)
1359 Broadway, Ste. 1509, New York, NY 10018
(212) 923-4700
fax: (212) 923-4778
website: www.pdf.org

The PDF is a nonprofit organization that is a leading national presence in Parkinson's disease research, education, and public advocacy. It funds promising scientific research while supporting people living with Parkinson's through educational programs and services. Its website includes downloadable archives of print newsletters, e-newsletters, and brochures as well as general information about the disease. It also offers online educational seminars.

Ride for Life
c/o Stony Brook
University, HSC, SSW
L2—Rm. 106, Stony
Brook, NY 11794
(631) 444-1292
fax: (631) 444-7565
e-mail@rideforlife.com
website: www.ridefor
life.com

Ride for Life is a nonprofit organization that aims to raise public awareness of ALS, assist researchers in finding a cure, support ALS patients and their families, and provide the ALS community with the latest ALS-related news and information. It conducts an annual ride during which ALS patients travel in their electric wheelchairs from one city to another. Its website contains information about the ride and other events as well as about its patient services.

University of California Institute for Memory Impairments and Neurological Disorders (UCI MIND)
2642 Biological
Sciences III, Irvine,
CA 92697-4545
(949) 824-3253
fax: 949-824-0885
website: www.alz.uci
.edu

UCI MIND seeks to conduct research to enhance the quality of life for the elderly by identifying factors and lifestyle approaches that promote successful brain aging. Among its activities is the training and education of graduate students and postdoctoral fellows in the field of brain aging and neurodegeneration. Its website contains information about the neurodegenerative disorders that most commonly affect older people.

FOR FURTHER READING

Books

Marjorie N. Allen, Susan Dublin, and P.J. Kimmerly, *A Look Inside Alzheimer's*. New York: Demos Health, 2012.

Walter G. Bradley, *Gib's Odyssey: One Man's Battle Against the Ravages of Lou Gehrig's Disease and His Courageous Final Voyage*. Guilford, CT: Lyons, 2012.

Philip Carlo, *The Killer Within: In the Company of Monsters*. New York: Overlook, 2011.

Patricia Farrell, *It's Not All in Your Head: Anxiety, Depression, Mood Swings, and Multiple Sclerosis*. New York: Demos Health, 2011.

Thomas Graboys, *Life in the Balance: A Physician's Memoir of Life, Love, and Loss with Parkinson's Disease and Dementia*. New York: Union Square, 2008.

Richard S. Isaacson, *Alzheimer's Treatment, Alzheimer's Prevention: A Patient and Family Guide*. Miami Beach: AD Education Consultants, 2012.

George Jelinek, *Overcoming Multiple Sclerosis: An Evidence-Based Guide to Recovery*. London: Allen and Unwin, 2010.

Rosalind C. Kalb, *Multiple Sclerosis: The Questions You Have, the Answers You Need*. New York: Demos Health, 2011.

Abraham Lieberman, *The Muhammad Ali Parkinson Center: 100 Questions & Answers About Parkinson Disease*. Sudbury, MA: Jones and Bartlett, 2009.

Judith London, *Connecting the Dots: Breakthroughs in Communication as Alzheimer's Advances*. Oakland, CA: New Harbinger, 2009.

Nancy L. Mace and Peter V. Rabins, *The 36-Hour Day: A Family Guide to Caring for People Who Have Alzheimer Disease, Related Dementias, and Memory Loss*. Baltimore: Johns Hopkins University Press, 2011.

Hiroshi Mitsumoto, ed., *Amyotrophic Lateral Sclerosis: A Guide for Patients and Families.* New York: Demos Health, 2009.

Michael S. Okun and Hubert H. Fernandez, *Ask the Doctor About Parkinson's Disease.* New York: Demos Health, 2009.

Nancy Pearce, *Inside Alzheimer's.* Taylors, SC: Forrason, 2011.

Oliver W.J. Quarrel, *Huntington's Disease: The Facts.* New York: Oxford University Press, 2008.

Morrie Schwartz, *Morrie: In His Own Words; Life Wisdom from a Remarkable Man.* New York: Walker, 2008.

Maria Shriver, *Alzheimer's in America: The Shriver Report on Women and Alzheimer's.* New York: Free Press, 2011.

William J. Weiner, Lisa M. Shulman, and Anthony E. Lang, *Parkinson's Disease: A Complete Guide for Patients and Families.* Baltimore: Johns Hopkins University Press, 2006.

Alice Wexler, *The Woman Who Walked into the Sea: Huntington's and the Making of a Genetic Disease.* New Haven, CT: Yale University Press, 2010.

Helen Buell Whitworth and Jim Whitworth, *A Caregiver's Guide to Lewy Body Dementia.* New York: Demos Health, 2010.

Periodicals and Internet Sources

Nicholas Bakalar, "First Mention: Lou Gehrig's Disease," *New York Times*, October 20, 2009.

Jeffrey Bartholet, "Controversy: Can Repeat Concussions Cause Lou Gehrig's Disease?," *Scientific American*, February 2012.

Dudley Clendinen, "The Good Short Life," *New York Times*, July 9, 2011.

Jamie DeSoto, "Copper Could Be the Culprit in Brain Disease," Center for Biomolecular Science and Engineering, January 11, 2010. https://cbse.soe.ucsc.edu/news/article/1782?ID=1782.

Disabled-World.com, "Stephen Hawking—A Journey Through Life," March 23, 2010. www.disabled-world.com/editorials/stephen-hawking.php.

Claudia Dreifus, "Life and the Cosmos, Word by Painstaking Word," *New York Times*, May 9, 2011.

EurekAlert, "New Guidelines Identify Best Treatments to Help ALS Patients Live Longer, Easier," October 12, 2009. www.eurekalert.org/pub_releases/2009-10/aaon-ngi100609.php.

———, "Smoking May Now Be Considered an Established Risk Factor for ALS, Also Known as Lou Gehrig's Disease," November 16, 2009. www.eurekalert.org/pub_releases/2009-11/bmc -smn111609.php.

Amy Harmon, "Fighting for a Last Chance at Life," *New York Times*, May 16, 2009.

Stephen Hawking, "Living with ALS." www.hawking.org.uk /living-with-als.html.

A . Hsu, "Juvenile Huntington's Disease," Huntington's Outreach Program for Education at Stanford, June 26, 2010. www .stanford.edu/group/hopes/cgi-bin/wordpress/category/hd -basics/juvenile-hd/.

Derrick Z. Jackson, "The Black Hole of Sports," *Boston Globe*, January 7, 2012. http://articles.boston.com/2012-01-07 /opinion/30601198_1_subconcussive-brain-banks-chronic -traumatic-encephalopathy.

Kristen Kersiek, "Infection and Neurodegenerative Diseases: Prions and Beyond," February 10, 2009. http://www.infection -research.de/perspectives/detail/pressrelease/infections_and _neurodegenerative_diseases_prions_and_beyond/.

Greg Miller, "Neurodegeneration: Could They All Be Prion Diseases?," *Science*, December 4, 2009.

Gretchen Morgenson, "From an Idea by Students, a Million-Dollar Charity," *New York Times*, November 11, 2009.

Brian Mossop, "Neurostress: How Stress May Fuel Neurodegenerative Diseases," *Scientific American*, February 2011. www .scientificamerican.com/article.cfm?id=neurostress-how-stress -ma.

Lauran Neergaard, "Scientists Uncover Culprit in Huntington's Disease," *Seattle Times*, June 4, 2009. http://seattletimes.nw source.com/html/health/2009300467_apusmedhuntingtons mystery.html.

NewsRx Health & Science, "Cigarette Smoking Associated with Increased Risk of Developing ALS," March 6, 2011. http://www.newsrx.com/health-articles/2378537.html.

NewsRx Health & Science, "New Treatment Helps Control Involuntary Crying and Laughing—Common in MS, ALS Patients," May 2, 2010. www.newsrx.com/health-articles/1892459.html.

Michael O'Donnell, "Solitary Confinement: Tony Judt Thought a Great Deal About Dignity: His Final Book, Written While the Author Was Dying of ALS, Is the Epitome of It," *Washington Monthly*, January/February 2011.

Alice Park, "Is Alzheimer's Caused by Contagious Proteins?," *Time*, February 3, 2012.

Sally Pobojewski, "When Neurons Die," *Medicine at Michigan*, Fall 2011. http://medicineatmichigan.com/magazine/2011/fall/neuronsdie/.

Ray Robinson, "70 Years Later, Gehrig's Speech Still Resonates with Inspiration," *New York Times*, June 27, 2009.

Denis Rodgerson, Ron Rothenberg, and Wayne A. Marasco, "New Hope for Curing Degenerative Diseases," *Life Extension Magazine*, October 2007. www.lef.org/magazine/mag2007/oct2007_report_stem_cells_01.htm.

Laura Sanders, "Young Man's Dreams, Old Man's Fate: Disorder Can Presage Neurodegenerative Disease by Decades," *Science News*, September 8, 2010.

George Vecsey, "Gehrig's Voice Echoes in a Story of Courage," *New York Times*, July 4, 2009.

Websites

Alzheimers Reading Room (www.alzheimersreadingroom.com). The Alzheimers Reading Room serves as a major source of news for the Alzheimer's community. Its goal is to educate, sometimes entertain, and always to empower Alzheimer's caregivers and their families, with a focus on the art of caregiving. It offers more than thirty-four hundred articles and stories.

INDEX